GRACE & SALT

12 BIBLICAL LESSONS TO TRANSFORM YOU AND YOUR TEAM INTO BETTER LEADERS

MELISSA MCCORMICK

MX3 BUSINESS SOLUTIONS

Grace & Salt: 12 Biblical Lessons to Transform You and Your Team into Better Leaders
by Melissa McCormick
Published by MX3 Business Solutions
www.graceandsaltbook.com

Print ISBN: 979-8-9853611-0-0
Ebook ISBN: 979-8-9853611-1-7

Editors & Proofreaders: Megan Ryan, Ginny Yttrup, Leslie McKee

Cover Design and interior graphics by Jenneth Dyck
jennethd1@gmail.com

Interior formatting by Ben Wolf
www.benwolf.com/editing-services

All Bible verses are from the NIV (1995), 10th anniversary edition, Zondervan unless otherwise noted. Used by permission.

Available in print and ebook format on amazon.com. Contact Melissa McCormick directly at melissa@graceandsaltbook.com for signed copies and to schedule author appearances and speaking events.

Copyright © 2021, 2022 by Melissa McCormick. All rights reserved. Non-commercial interests may reproduce portions of this book without the express written permission of the author, provided the text does not exceed 500 words. For longer quotations or commercial concerns, please email the author at melissa@graceandsaltbook.com.

Commercial interests: No part of this publication may be reproduced in any form, stored in a retrieval system, or transmitted in any form by any means—electronic, photocopy, recording, or otherwise—without prior written permission of the author, except as provided by the United States of America copyright law. All book links within this work are Amazon affiliate links.

This is a work of nonfiction. Any mentioned brand names, characters, places, and trademarks remain the property of their respective owners, bear no association with the author or the publisher, and are used for fictional purposes only. Any similarities to individuals living or dead is purely coincidental. Printed in the United States of America.

WHAT ARE THE EXPERTS SAYING?

Melissa McCormick has an amazing leadership story herself. From a very humble career beginning, she ultimately became a strong corporate leader with global responsibilities, in an era where being a woman was often unfortunately another career hurdle to overcome. She continues her journey today providing inspiration and guidance to young and aspiring leaders through her community and civic outreach and business consulting.

In her book Grace & Salt, Melissa crystalizes a lifetime of career and leadership experience in a single creative volume. The book provides a very enlightening overview of Melissa's servant-leadership perspective in a series of lessons that address practical business situations that all leaders face. These lessons are presented in the context of spiritual quotes from the Bible, and they provide excellent common-sense skills and techniques that will help anyone interested in growing their leadership capability. Whether seen through the Biblical lens, or seen strictly from the business perspective, this book is an outstanding resource for leaders at any level of their personal development.

– Dave Boden, President/CEO, Hiway Credit Union

I have been looking forward to reading this book. Since I have known the author throughout most of her professional career, I was anxious to learn more about the ways she was able to so successfully unite her family life with her professional life. I knew that her spiritual life had a great deal to do with that, but now I know that Jesus Christ was at the core of all aspects of her life. I now know how intently she listened to the direction He gave her in prayer. This is a compelling and honest description of a sincere person's life, intentionally lived in harmony with Christ her Lord and Savior.

– Joe Barrett, CEO, Barrett Trade & Finance Company

Grace & Salt is a collection of carefully developed and selected leadership tools; including real-life scenarios, poignant bible verses and parables, self-awareness exercises, and sound leadership advice from a corporate veteran and faithful Christian, Melissa McCormick. This book provides insights on how to apply the correct amount of candor (salt) with the right blend of compassion and understanding (grace) to business and/or personal situations. Applying these insights to business or personal interactions provides an opportunity to deepen relationships, better understanding others, and greater inner peace. Grace & Salt is a timely arrival for individuals and management teams who are looking to take things to the next level - without scrimping on morals, and who are genuinely interested in treating themselves and others with better intentions, care, and concern.

— **Melissa Wolfe, Owner, Foster Brands, LLC**

Sometimes the fear of the unknown is the obstacle to help us grow in all areas of life. Grace & Salt taught me to trust my inner strength to speak up and step out of my comfort zone. For anyone who wants to learn more about developing themself and building strong teams, I highly recommend this book.

— **Tricia Bennett, Sr. Director Program Management, Taylor Company**

For some, wisdom comes through experience. They have to learn through their own experiences of failure, difficulty, and setback. However, Godly wisdom is found in also gleaning from the experiences of others. This book is the perfect tool for those seeking the latter. Melissa McCormick serves her readers by sharing the lessons learned in her decades of leadership. However, despite her business success, she chooses to share from a posture of humility, vulnerable and transparency. This makes these lessons and examples relatable to anyone.

What she learned, and what she points her readers' attention to, is the truth of biblical wisdom, clearly stated in the pages of scripture, that fits perfectly the contexts of everyday business relationships.

I was both encouraged and challenged by this book and I am confident that you will be as well.

— **Wayne Hume, Senior Pastor, Northeast Christian Church**

*I dedicate this book to my husband, Mike, who inspired me to write this book
and has been right beside me every step of this journey.*

*To my children, Amanda and Nick,
who believe in me even when I don't believe in myself.*

*And to my mom who has taught me (us)
to stand strong, be strong, and to live strong.*

CONTENTS

Foreword	1
Preface	3

SECTION I: GRACE & SALT LEADERSHIP

Lesson I: Grace & Salt	15
Lesson II: Connections & Sense of Belonging	29
Lesson III: Serving & Giving	45
Lesson IV: Remove Inactive Yeast Swiftly	63
Lesson V: Planting Seeds & Fishing	79
Lesson VI: Pray Until Something Happens (PUSH)	103
Section I: Grace & Salt Leadership Summary	109

SECTION II – THE LEADER — HOW TO MAINTAIN AND SURVIVE THE CHAOS

Lesson VII: Temptation — Use Your Power for Good	115
Lesson VIII: Courage — Be Like Esther: Stand Up, Speak Up, and Step Out	141
Lesson IX: Refresh Yourself — Have a SPA (Spiritual Personal Activity) Day!	149
Lesson X: Self-Awareness & Growth — The New You	155
Lesson XI: Mentor - Have One, Be One	167
Lesson XII: The Power of Prayer in Leadership	177
Section II: The Leader: How to Maintain and Survive the Chaos Summary	181
Closing Thoughts	183
My Story	185
Endnotes	193
Acknowledgments	197
About the Author	201

FOREWORD

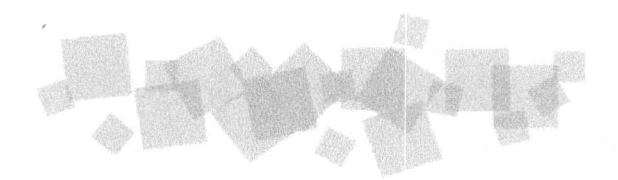

I have known Melissa McCormick for more than 20 years. We met at the company where she devoted most of her professional career. I have watched as she excelled in every way: expanding the company's sales globally, taking on an increasingly broad array of responsibilities, becoming a key member of the executive management team. Through it all, she encouraged employees and clients alike to be the best that they could be.

She always exhibited strength of character and clarity of purpose.

This book answers many questions I had as to how she was able to function so well in this highly competitive and, for most of her years with this company, a male-dominated environment.

Through it all, she maintained her integrity, drive, and convictions. That Jesus Christ was at the core of her strength is no surprise. What was exhilarating to read was how that relationship with Him played out every day in her life and career.

This is a must-read for anyone who strives to unite all aspects of life: family, professional, and spiritual.

Joseph T. Barrett, President
Barrett Trade & Finance Group

PREFACE

Welcome to Grace & Salt. This book is filled with lessons for leaders. Leaders who lead others and leaders who lead without direct employees. Over the past thirty years, these lessons became part of my leadership style and I'm excited to share them with you.

Through these lessons you'll see how God helped me navigate the workplace and taught me to listen to His messengers. You see, my story is where God's messengers showed up in my life. It's how I listened to God through them. This book is a fulfillment of my promise to share these lessons with you so that you can benefit from them.

We're all leaders whether we lead direct employees or not. Leadership is a choice. Don't get me wrong, there's a time for following but I'll save that for another book. These lessons are rooted in my faith in Jesus and His purpose for me.

How this book came to life

In 2014, I was the vice president of sales for the Americas at a foodservice equipment manufacturing company while balancing family responsibilities and a youth director role at our church. The youth director was responsible for organizing and leading the annual student mission trips. The mission trips led us from Colorado to South Carolina and everywhere in between. Although the trips were intended to bring the students closer to Jesus, they improved my relationship with Him, as well. They allowed time for God to show me and lead me toward His purpose.

On the last night of each mission trip, the students and trip leaders reflect on how the trip's experiences have impacted their relationships with Jesus. The main focus of the trip is to serve local communities and to apply the lessons learned to the communities and neighborhoods back home.

Oklahoma memory

Oklahoma sure is hot and humid no matter if it's day or night. Tonight was no different. The worship service was full of energy and exhilarating. Reality was about to hit. We're leaving tomorrow to head back home.

I step back and watch the kids. Shawn and Amanda are talking, and Nick and Bryson are kidding around.

"Okay. Let's circle up and have some church time," I said. "Well, it's been a long week, and we've worked really hard. You should be proud of yourselves for the tons of painting and cleaning you did and the relationships you made at the nursing home. I want you to think about the week and your experiences. When you're ready, share with us how you'll apply the lessons back home."

Did I tell them to look at their shoes? The humid night air is thick and uncomfortable. Dogs barking in the night and no one saying a word. *Are they thinking or delaying? After all, they are teenagers.* Time is standing still.

Finally, Ethan asks, "What are *you* going to do with what *you* learned?"

Perfect. That's just like Ethan, to answer a question with a question. But it's a fair one.

Glaring at him with a "mom look," I said, "That's fair."

Thinking about it for a few minutes, I said, "Well, each day when I drive to work, I pray for the day, for church, for blessings, for friends and family. But when I get to work, I park my car, open the door, and lock Jesus in the passenger seat. I think I need to bring Jesus to work with me.

"Here's my commitment to each of you. Starting Monday morning, I'll bring my Bible to work and read it first thing when I get there. Then, we'll see how it goes."

The discussions continue until each student shared their plans.

For the next year, I read for five to ten minutes each morning before my day started. After reading, I prayed for the company, the interactions in my office, the leadership team, the decisions we faced, and that God was at the center of all decisions.

I wrote down any Bible verse that touched my heart or was applicable to a situation I faced. Most nights, I came home and told my husband about a Bible verse I read in the morning and a situation it applied to in the afternoon.

One evening driving home from dinner, I told him another story of how a Bible verse applied to a work situation.

Mike said, "You should really write a book."

"What?" I thought he was crazy.

"No, really. This is good stuff and you should share it."

I thought about it for weeks. *OK. If Mike thinks it's a good idea, then I will.* I know it sounds odd but God usually speaks to me through Mike. He's right. These leadership lessons from Jesus, Esther, Nicodemus, Paul, and others are important and need to be shared.

I continued to read the Bible at work, write in my journal, and think of this book at church, while driving in the car, at work, and every place I went. Honestly, it consumed me.

Grace & Salt takes shape

In November of 2015, while in Spain on business, I took a few vacation days to concentrate on the book. I lived and studied in Spain during college, and spending time at Jardines De La Reina in Marbella was the perfect bed-and-breakfast to figure out what's next.

Arriving early in the morning, I rent a car and start my trek to Marbella. The trip is longer than anticipated especially because I stop every hour to call the States to keep me awake.

What a beautiful drive through the countryside. Farmland and windmills dot the landscape. *Hey, is that Don Quixote and Sancho Panza riding donkeys over the hills, or am I hallucinating due to fatigue?* If you aren't familiar with Don Quixote, search Google images or read the book. It's a pretty good read if you enjoy old books and crazy stories.

Spending time focused on my book and sightseeing are exactly what I need.

Finally, there's the sign. I've arrived in Marbella.

The road winds up the mountainside, and my driving skills are tested as I maneuver the narrow roadways. The entrance to Jardines De La Reina is narrow. I slowly turn the car between two whitewashed concrete barriers into the small parking area. The bed-and-breakfast is beautiful. Spanish tiled roof and curvy white walls of the house.

"Hi! Welcome to Jardines. I'm Diego, the owner. Let me help you with your luggage and show you to your room."

"Perfect. I'm exhausted."

Bright orange, purple, and red silk and chiffon fabric drape the ceiling and room. A dark mahogany four-poster bed sits in the center of the room with brightly colored pillows and silk fabric draped around the posters. The large bathroom has a Spanish-tiled floor and walls. It's the perfect location to focus on writing this book.

Each morning I wake up to the sunrise and eat breakfast in the outdoor patio next to the pool. After breakfast, the next few hours are spent sitting on my bed with my notes, journal, and computer. I'm looking for a theme, and additional research helps develop the idea, thought, or lesson.

Right around lunch time, it's time to explore and drive along the coast. It's relaxing to stop spontaneously in little seaside towns and enjoy the ocean or watch the sunset. The funny thing is that parallel parking isn't in my vocabulary so I keep driving until I find a parking space where I can pull straight in. If you've been to Europe, you know that parallel parking is essential. A few times, the two-lane round-a-bouts catch me off guard when I need to exit and I'm in the inside lane. Spanish drivers are considerate and give me space and grace.

Going off the grid leaves me refreshed and renewed. The main goal for the Marbella trip is to organize my notes and see if anything is there. Is there a theme, or are my notes simply a random collection of thoughts? Is there enough for a book or only a blog? My goal is to develop an outline by Monday when I travel back to Madrid for a business meeting. And that's what I did.

Leaving Marbella with an outline is thrilling. The book outline focuses on leadership lessons that I incorporate into my own leadership style and thoughts on how to survive the chaos of being a leader.

Hearing God

It blows me away how God spoke through my husband and how he became one of God's messengers. We married in my childhood church and both believed in Jesus but didn't pray together or talk about our faith until later in our marriage. If you're married, maybe you can relate to this type of relationship. I was active in our church, but faith and Jesus didn't come up in our conversations until I shared with him the leadership lessons I learned through daily Bible reading.

Prior to writing this book, I struggled with knowing how to hear God. I'd hear sermons on listening to God, but if God didn't write me a letter directly, I wasn't sure how to hear him. Now, I know. He sends His messengers and speaks through His Word.

For the next several years, focusing on writing was inconsistent.

Satan didn't want this book to be published. He kept me busy with work and life, which became distractions from God's purpose.

In 2016, Dan Domberg came into my life. Dan applied for a job and during the interview process, he told me he was a member of Northeast Christian Church. My husband and I attend the same church. I didn't know it at the time but God sent another messenger to encourage me. Dan became a friend, supporter, and colleague. He gently pushed me to continue to write and not give up.

In 2018, on a mission trip to the Dominican Republic through Northeast Christian Church, God introduced me to Megan Ryan. Megan is a book editor. Another messenger God put in my path.

The point I'm making is that God put specific people in my path relating to the writing and publishing of this book. I was aware of what was happening and could feel God opening a door for me or *pushing* me through it. Would I walk through it? Would I follow His purpose? Would I listen to Him and His messengers?

Finish the book, already!

Later that year, God pushed me to finish the book and tell my story. So, after late-night discussions with my husband and a lot of introspection, I made a big decision and decided to leave my company, Taylor Company, after thirty-two years of service.

Taylor is like "Hotel California" from the Eagles song. "You can check out but you can never leave." Employees leave but they typically return. Even if you don't, the company, employees, customers, distributors, and products are always at the forefront of your mind and thoughts. It's a special place that's difficult to explain unless you experience it.

Well, it was time to leave "Hotel California." Leave my comfort zone and walk through the door God opened. There are many examples of how God put people in my path to show me His purpose for the second half of my life. I've included the details in my story at the end of this book.

My hope

My hope is this book provides clear and concise leadership lessons rooted in Jesus. I wrote this book for two reasons: to fulfill God's will and share the lessons.

This interactive book includes evaluation exercises and thought-provoking questions to help evaluate your team and your own leadership style. The answers to the questions and evaluations won't be given to you. They come through your own introspection and reflection.

Welcome to my story. I hope you enjoy this interactive experience.

SECTION I: GRACE & SALT LEADERSHIP

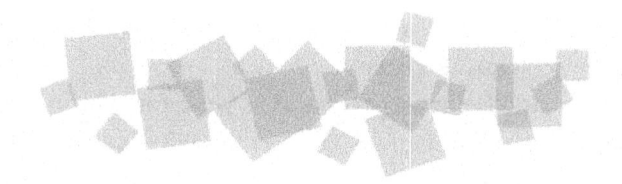

It's 7:30 a.m. and busy at work. Working in the international side of the business means that by 7:30, my inbox is full. Not an e-mail inbox. This is the 80s.

Reams of paper spill over the back of the telex machine, and faxes are strewn all over the floor. Picking them up and sorting them is my responsibility.

I wasn't given the job. I just took it and started doing it because it felt right. Who wants to have papers all over the floor?

Well, since I started doing it, it became my responsibility. It's funny how those things happen.

Sitting at my desk I sort the messages for emergencies. This is a typical day.

Employees drift into the office, and the hustle and bustle begins. Telephones ring, keyboards click, and muffled conversations are heard in the coffee room.

As the supervisor, customers and shipments are my primary focus. My day speeds along.

What? More faxes to sort!

Will we make our shipment quota today?

Of course, I'll take care of the customer complaint. Transfer the call.

Hello? No, she's not at her desk. What do you need?

Of course, I'll type the fax and send it for you.

Production manager, are all of our shipments shipping today?

Whew. It's 5:00 already?

I like my job and feel valuable, but I want more. From the first day on the job, my dream was to advance to vice president of international sales. I want to make an impact on the company and our customers.

Truth be told, I also want to make more money. Being a value and money are big motivators for me.

After four years as the supervisor, it's time for a promotion. Maybe, if I keep working hard and taking care of the office, someone will notice.

Fifty to sixty hours a week aren't unusual, and I like being the "go-to" person. *I'm sure that any moment my boss will call me into his office and tell me I'm being promoted to a manager or director.*

Time passes slowly. I continue to work hard. *Maybe it's time to focus on my family and a promotion will come later.*

Two children and four years later.

Oh. There's a new job posting for the marketing department. Sounds interesting. It's a lateral move but will be different. I'm so bored.

"Hello? Of course, I'll be right down."

That's fantastic. I GOT THE JOB!

International marketing is fun and exciting. Pretty soon, I know someone will tell me how valuable I am and will lead me to the vice president job.

Ten – fourteen - nineteen years pass and I haven't shared my career goals.

Gathering enough courage, I call my boss. "Hi, Jeremy. Do you have a moment? I'd like to talk to you about my career goals."

Welcome to Grace & Salt

The lessons discussed in this book are those I learned as I advanced through the company.

My story

I began working at Taylor Company on November 9, 1987, as a bilingual documents clerk. By the way, I hated that title. Who wants to be called a "clerk"? The title didn't properly describe or acknowledge the responsibilities of the role. Once I became the department supervisor, I changed the title to "international inside sales & logistics."

I graduated from Luther College with a bachelor's degree in Spanish and a minor in psychology. Speaking Spanish was my ultimate goal. Four years later, I accepted a supervisory role to fill a vacancy. I transitioned from co-worker to mid-level manager overnight. My career path winded upwards and sideways until I hit the "glass ceiling." *Could this be true? Does the glass ceiling exist?* Yes, ladies and gentlemen, it does. But not because someone was holding me down but because I didn't speak up. Again, I thought if I worked hard, someone would notice and *they* would take control of *my* career.

Getting out of the Career Comfort Zone

"Hi, Jeremy. Do you have a moment? I'd like to talk to you about my career goals."

It was time to take control of my career and speak up. Speaking up was critical. The minute I told my boss my goals, he took an active role in my career plan and guided me forward. It wasn't linear and it wasn't easy, but action was required. Over the next ten years, I received roles of director of sales, vice president of sales—the Americas, and finally, my favorite, the senior vice president of global sales, service, and marketing. The reason I'm telling you my career path is to provide context and credibility to the lessons in this book.

Grace & Salt

There are two sections in this book.

The first section, Grace & Salt Leadership, creates a leadership development plan for you and your team. It includes an evaluation of your leadership style and skills and those of your team.

The second section, How to Maintain and Survive the Chaos, focuses on the leader specifically and how to survive the chaos of leadership.

There are interactive exercises and time for introspection. I draw on my professional and personal experience in each lesson. This book inspires critical thinking, application, and growth. When you're finished, you'll have an analysis of your leadership style, your team members, and a development plan to create a culture of connections, sense of belonging, community, and accountability.

Grace & Salt leadership requires intentionality in five core areas, including courage, communication, connections, community [serving and giving to others], and self-care. You'll see these five leadership components incorporated throughout this book.

We begin with communication, a core component, in the first lesson, Grace & Salt. Communication is the cornerstone to all relationships. If you can learn how to master strong communication skills rooted in respect for others, you'll handle any challenge that comes your way. Trust me and enjoy!

LESSON I: GRACE & SALT

*Let your conversation be always full of grace, seasoned with salt,
so that you may know how to answer everyone.*
Colossians 4:6

*E*arly in my career, I sat at my desk one Monday morning, surrounded by international orders for machines and parts I was responsible to ship. Just gathering the documentation required for international shipping felt like a full-time job, but that was just the beginning of the tasks I was responsible for in the order entry department.

That morning, I held the phone to my ear and listened to the postal worker I'd called for information on a particular shipment, shaking my head as he spoke. *No, that's not how it works.* My grip on the phone tightened. *No, no, no.*

Finally, I interrupted, "No. You're wrong. I've done this dozens of times. That's not how it works." My tone was brusque, but he was wrong. I didn't have time to waste—I had a job to do.

I ended the call and proceeded with the task. A few minutes later, my phone rang. Multi-tasking, I picked it up and continued with what I was doing. I stilled when the caller identified himself as the CFO of our company. He proceeded to ask me about the conversation I'd just had with the postal worker.

How'd he know?

I explained the circumstance, my perception of the situation, and my reaction to the postal worker.

His response has stayed with me all these years. He said, "You know, Melissa, I understand, but sometimes you can get more flies with honey than vinegar."

I'd come to find out later that the postal worker and the CFO were friends, and the postal worker had contacted him right after our abrupt exchange.

I learned an important lesson that day...

Honey and vinegar

Good advice. If you've never heard that saying before, it means you'll make more friends by treating others with respect or "sweetness" [honey] than with rudeness [vinegar]. Immaturity may have contributed to my response as well as my personality. Being a police officer's daughter taught me the difference between right and wrong. To me, it's simple: when it's right, it's right, and when it's wrong, it's wrong. I'm sure that if I had used more honey than vinegar, the postal worker would've become a friend rather than avoiding him for years.

Fast forward more than twenty years and I read Colossians 4:6. Paul tells us to be full of grace and seasoned with salt or truth. Grace & Salt are similar to the honey and vinegar advice I received years before. It was an "a-ha" moment where the lightbulb went off. I grew to lead with Grace & Salt but didn't understand the concept fully until I truly incorporated it into my leadership and communication styles.

Paul's instructions

In Colossians, Paul, the apostle, instructs the Colossians to always give thanks to God. He gives them three instructions. First, change their behavior. Second, give their lives to Christ, and third, live for Christ rather than for themselves.

He says, *"...clothe yourselves with compassion, kindness, humility, gentleness and patience. Bear with each other and forgive whatever grievances you may have against one another. Forgive as the Lord forgave you"*. Col. 3:12-13

Applying Paul's instructions to leadership is powerful. Treat your team members and colleagues with forgiveness, gentleness, and patience. Yes, this is easier said than done. Patience and gentleness are difficult when there is a business to run.

You might be thinking:

- "But customers are screaming for answers."
- "How can I possibly treat others with gentleness and patience when the corporate office is breathing down my neck?"
- "My number one priority is to meet our financial goals and not whether I hurt my employee's feelings."

If these statements resonate with you, I'm not suggesting your leadership style should be soft, weak, and accepting of poor performance. I am suggesting we follow Paul's instructions.

Grace & Salt

Full of grace and seasoned with salt. Before we jump to conclusions, fill yourself with patience and gentleness, and listen to understand through the eyes of grace.

Grace

What is grace? To me, the definition of grace is to give forgiveness to the undeserved. Offering forgiveness to someone who didn't meet a deadline for an important project or offering forgiveness (grace) to an employee who is late for work.

To listen to understand through the eyes of grace is to acknowledge and

EVERYONE HAS A STORY.

accept that everyone has a story. It's to offer grace to someone whose life "got in the way" of the expectations.

It also means to fully and actively listen to understand *before* responding. Listen to the words *and* the body language. What emotions are being portrayed through the discussion? The tone of voice, the location of their arms and hands, facial expressions, and gestures. Listen with your ears and *your eyes*.

Salt

Conversations should be "seasoned with salt." Salt in this context means truth.[1] The intent to add salt or truth to each conversation is to teach, get better, and resolve a situation and not to hurt, harm, or criticize.

Historically, salt preserved meat and was used as currency in Egypt.[2] It had great importance in the old world. Today, it's used to heal wounds, tan leather, keep wicker looking new, remove wine from carpet, and clean grease stains from rugs.[3]

The point is that salt is used primarily for preservation and removing stains; truth can be used for

◆ SALT IS TRUTH.

preservation and removing stains as well. According to Tisdale, "Salt is as free as the water suspending it when it's dissolved and as immutable as stone when it is dry."[4]

Let's take a moment to picture that. Take a glass of water and pour salt into it. What happens? Imagine it floating in the water to the bottom of the glass. Have you ever made salt water? In order for the water to absorb the salt, stir it or shake it a bit. All of the salt isn't absorbed. The rest slowly floats and suspends for a few seconds as it finds its way to the bottom of the glass. "Salt is as free as the water suspending it when it's dissolved."

It's also as "immutable as stone when it is dry." Think about a block of salt. Have you seen a salt lick for animals? How about using Himalayan salt blocks for cooking steak or salmon? These salt blocks are hard as rock and difficult to break. To break a block of salt without heating it you need a hammer, chisel, and, sometimes, a drill.

Truth is similar in relationships. If truth is delivered with a balance of grace, it is as free as the salt floating to the bottom of a glass. It offers freedom and improves relationships. However, if truth is not balanced with grace, it can turn relationships to stone like a block of salt.

Balance and blending

The key word is balance. Balance indicates a 50/50 split, but most agree this isn't realistic. In this context, balance refers to the right amount of grace with the right amount of salt.

You may be wondering, how much salt or grace do I add?

Well, it depends on the situation and the person. The only constant in leadership is each situation is different. Most of the answers begin with "it depends." This is one reason why listening to understand is so important.

Regardless of the amount of salt, don't forget to wrap your words in grace (kindness, understanding, listening).

When I spoke to the postal worker, I used too much salt and didn't wrap it in an ounce of grace. I was blunt and quite frankly rude. In that situation, salt was important because I felt the postal worker's information was incorrect but grace was more important.

Original response: Finally, I interrupted, "No. You're wrong. I've done this dozens of times. That's not how it works."

This response had 100% salt and 0% grace. My mistake was that I didn't weigh the importance of our relationship into my response. I told him exactly what I thought and how he was wrong.

In those days, international shipping required frequent visits to the post office and having a good relationship with the postal workers made my job easier.

Revised response wrapped with grace: Finally, I interrupted, "I see. Okay. Are you sure that's how I complete the documentation? The reason I'm questioning is that I was told previously to complete the papers differently."

This response is wrapped in grace because I asked if he was sure of the information but also included salt because it explained what I had been told in the past.

What conversations have you had recently? Was more grace needed or more salt?

COVID-19, a Time of Crisis

Workforce reductions and budget cuts are difficult decisions to make. The COVID-19 global pandemic is a good example. It forced companies to make difficult decisions swiftly.

In the United States, over 16 million people were unemployed, and businesses were shut down at the height of the pandemic. The government ordered all residents to shelter in place and to only go out for essential items, i.e., food, medicine, supplies.

How many of you faced tough decisions to lay off employees or furlough them for 30, 60 or 90 days?

If you are an executive team member and made those decisions, remember the emotions you felt during the decision-making process.

Think about the difficult discussions with your employees on the state of the company. What was their response and the emotions shared? Remembering and learning from the experience teaches valuable lessons on how to address future crises.

What went right and what went wrong? What lessons did we learn to not repeat in the future? It also reminds us to be joyful when the situation is history.

On the other hand, it's possible that your company thrived during COVID-19. Hospitals, nurses, and doctors worked day and night to help patients recover. Face masks, face shields, and protective gown manufacturers produced at record levels to fill the pipeline with critical equipment.

In both situations, stress and anxiety increased during those times. What was the stress and anxiety like for you?

The challenge that you or your leaders may have faced to balance keeping the business open and people employed was probably staggering.

Typically, the general employee doesn't know these discussions take place. However, in the case of COVID-19, everyone knew.

Using Grace & Salt under stress

The pandemic created stress in all levels of the workforce. The general worker who worried about their job. The manager who worried about job performance or provided names of possible layoff candidates. The executive who worried about making workforce reduction decisions.

Grace & Salt is a communication technique that reminds you to put the stress of the day aside and listen to the person speaking. To be totally present.

The higher you are in the organization, the more important the concept of Grace & Salt becomes. Stress is difficult to manage at all levels of a company, but the spotlight shines brightest on those in high levels or corner offices.

> **TIP**: Incorporate *Grace & Salt*, G&S, into your daily routine. Let it become your go-to phrase. These letters, G&S, remind you to force the daily issues and stress to the back of your mind and focus on who is in front of you.

Remembering the Grace & Salt technique is best for the person(s) you're leading, but also, it's best for you. Grace & Salt is a powerful concept and one we should master, especially during times of crisis. Let's spend time digging deeper into the lesson.

Leading with grace

When leading with grace, words of kindness and understanding are used rather than words of hurt and criticism. Offering grace doesn't mean we ignore difficult conversations and give the employee a pass for a wrongdoing.

It does mean that everyone has a story, and before jumping to conclusions, listen to understand first. Listen for what is behind the behavior.

Leading with grace scenario

It's 8:15 when Jim arrives. His supervisor notices but decides not to say anything. *Probably a rough morning. He's always on time.*

Jim leaves the office when his shift ends without saying goodbye. *That's odd. He usually lets me know when he's leaving.*

The following day, Jim rolls into the office ten minutes late and saunters into his cubicle.

Again, that's odd. I wonder if something is wrong, his supervisor thinks.

This pattern continues for a few days.

The supervisor peers over Jim's cubicle wall. "Hey, Jim, I've noticed you've been late for work all week. Is something wrong at home?"

"Nope. Everything's fine."

"Hmm. Okay. Well, please remember your shift starts at 8:00."

The next week, Jim's behavior continues. He's late most of the week.

Finally, the supervisor calls him into her office. "Jim, I'm concerned about the sudden change in tardiness. You're typically on time, but yet the last few weeks you've been showing up ten to fifteen minutes late most days. What's going on?" [The supervisor is listening to understand.]

"Well, honestly, I've noticed Sue is late all the time, and it seems okay. So, I thought it didn't matter when I showed up. I've been taking my time getting to work. It really frustrates me that you're talking to me and not to Sue!"

The supervisor explains to Jim that she can't discuss details of Sue's situation but assured him it was being handled. There isn't a double standard and received confirmation from Jim that he would be on time for work going forward.

What did the supervisor do right? The supervisor talked to Jim to prevent the situation from getting out of control. Their discussion showed that Jim was already disengaging due to the perceived double standard.

If Jim feels this way, do other employees agree with him? Is the department's morale falling? This is something to consider.

The best course of action is to address the situation early and focus on the behavior. The supervisor began the discussion from a position of grace.

She started with "I'm concerned" and asked him to give her his side of the story. She didn't make assumptions of what was behind the behavior.

> **TIP:** Communicate with the team on changes to the team's policies or schedules. This avoids hard feelings or perceptions of favoritism.

If needed, find a compromise for both the employee and the company that is within company guidelines, of course. Whatever the outcome, it's important to communicate with the rest of the team and advise them of the reason behind the change without divulging personal information.

Leading with *too* much grace

Jim's supervisor led with grace, but what happens when we lead with too much grace? What if the supervisor hates conflict? A supervisor who avoids conflict and doesn't address poor performance directly leads with a "beating around the bush" leadership style.

Most people avoid conflict, and supervisors are no different, but it can be detrimental to the team when a supervisor ignores poor behavior.

Let's look at a similar example where the supervisor demonstrates "beating around the bush" leadership.

"Beating around the bush" scenario

"Hi Jane, how's everything at home?" the supervisor asks walking into Jane's office.

Jane looks up from her computer, a bit surprised by the question. "Um. Fine. Everyone's great. Thanks for asking."

"Great. Hey, I was wondering if something is going on at home since you arrived a few minutes late this morning."

"Nope. Everything's good," Jane said, and the supervisor left the room. *That was nice of him to ask about my family. I love working for a boss who cares.*

What happened? Instead of clearly identifying the supervisor's expectations of being on time, the supervisor talked around the situation or "beat around the bush."

From the supervisor's perspective, they were uncomfortable having the discussion and hoped the employee understood the underlying message.

From Jane's perspective, she appreciated their concern and continued to arrive late.

Unfortunately, both the underperforming employee, Jane, and her team members were impacted. Jane wasn't provided with information to help her understand the expectations. Instead, she thinks she works for a caring supervisor. The message Jane received was that being late wasn't a big deal because her supervisor didn't tell her the behavior needed to change nor did he explain the expectations.

Jane's team members were impacted because they know Jane is late and they may perceive a double standard.

Let's look at how the supervisor could have handled the discussion by blending grace and salt.

The supervisor could have said something like this: "Jane, I've noticed you've been late to work recently. I'm sure you understand that being on time is part of the job. Is there something going on?"

By starting the conversation with a softer approach, it's obvious that you are giving the employee an opportunity to tell their side of the story before continuing. The supervisor led with grace but included salt (truth) in the direct approach.

This removes the chance of misinterpretation for the reason behind the discussion and the expectations. The supervisor clearly said, "being on time is part of the job."

However, beginning the sentence with "I'm sure you understand…" softens the statement and removes an accusatory tone. The employee doesn't become defensive. The salt is wrapped with grace.

Employees and too much grace

Employees who don't approach each other or their supervisors when issues arise extend too much grace.

Perhaps a colleague launches a new marketing campaign without communicating the details to your department, and you're responsible to tally the customers' responses. Your plate is full with two campaigns pending, and you struggle with the additional workload.

Rather than talk to the co-worker, you decide to work overtime and hope it doesn't happen again. Odds are it will happen again.

The best course of action is to address it early regardless of the perceived conflict. The colleague needs to understand the impact of their decision.

Both supervisors and employees benefit from incorporating grace & salt communication techniques into their communication styles.

Listen to understand, blend the right amount of grace & salt, and wrap the salt with grace.

It's time to practice dealing with conflicts.

CONFLICT AVOIDANCE EXERCISE

STEP ONE: Identify an example when you avoided a discussion and extended too much grace. If you can't think of an example, review the questions below:

- Think about each member on your team and ask: Have I avoided a conversation with this person and if so, why?
- If you don't have team members, think about a colleague or family member that you have interacted with in the past week or month and ask yourself the same question: Have I avoided a conversation with this person and if so, why?
- Look at your calendar over the past month to refresh your memory. What meetings or conference calls took place? Did you choose to avoid a discussion or didn't bring up a topic because it was controversial?

STEP TWO: Use the example identified to answer the following questions. Write your responses in your journal.

What was the situation? (Provide a full description.)
Who was it with?
Why did I avoid the discussion?
Have I avoided discussions with this person in the past?
If so, how many times?
How should I have handled it?
What will I do next time a similar situation arises?

JOURNAL EXERCISE EVALUATION

Take a look at your responses.

- What trends do you notice?
- Who do you avoid conflict with or offer too much grace?
- Have you led with too much grace multiple times with different people?
- Are you a leader that avoids conflict?

STEP THREE: Create a plan. Literally, write down a plan to improve avoiding conflict.

To help with this exercise, download the worksheet, Overcoming Conflict Avoidance Plan, at www.graceandsaltbook.com/resources.

Balancing or blending constructive conversations with Grace & Salt allows the employee to grow in their development and strengthens your relationship.

The leader, employee, and company benefit in the long term. Practice incorporating Grace & Salt into every conversation at work and at home.

Lesson I: As you go through your everyday life, fill your conversations with G & S.

Let your conversation be always full of grace, seasoned with salt, so that you may know how to answer everyone. Colossians 4:6

Blend grace & salt based on the circumstances and relationship with the other person(s). And wrap the conversation in grace regardless of the amount of salt needed.

FIVE STEPS TO IMPLEMENT GRACE & SALT INTO DIFFICULT CONVERSATIONS.

STEP ONE: Identify an example where you avoid a conversation. Journal about the discussion using these questions:

- What was the situation? (Provide a full description)
- Who was it with?
- Why did I avoid the discussion?
- Have I avoided discussions with this person in the past?
- If so, how many times?
- How should I have handled it?
- Finally, what will I do next time a similar situation arises?

STEP TWO: Identify trends with specific person(s) or situation/topic.

STEP THREE: Establish an action plan the next time this situation arises.

STEP FOUR: Record the outcome on the Grace & Salt journal page (download at www.graceandsaltbook.com/resouces). Recording the outcome of each interaction on a journal page shows progress and accountability.

STEP FIVE: Celebrate successes including moments when you addressed a difficult situation or person. Adjust the plan and approach as needed after each discussion.

LESSON II: CONNECTIONS & SENSE OF BELONGING

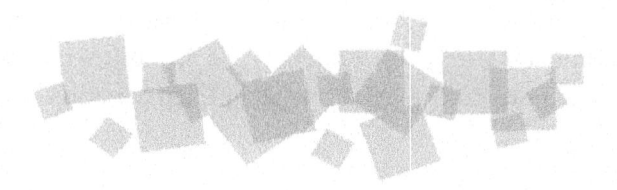

To the weak I became weak, to win the weak. I have become all things to all people so that by all possible means I might save some.
1 Corinthians 9:22

It's early Monday morning when Tricia stops by to check in.

"Hey, how was the weekend? Feeling, okay?"

"It was quiet. Spent most of the time with Amanda. I'm so tired. This baby takes every ounce of energy."

"I can imagine."

"How do you think this outfit looks? I bought this suit jacket at Salvation Army in a bigger size to hide my stomach. Does it work?"

"Absolutely, but it might be time to tell your employees. I'm guessing you have a few weeks before you'll need maternity clothes."

"I know. I'm dreading it. Remember what happened when I was pregnant with Amanda? I told everyone at twelve weeks, and they all thought my stomach was public property. I know it's been six months, but I really don't want to go through that again. Lunch today?"

"Please!"

This conversation is fiction, but the situation is true. I waited six months before I told my co-workers and staff that I was pregnant. Throughout most of my career, I didn't understand the point in personal conversations with co-workers. After all, *we have a business to run.*

I came to work, did my job, and went home. I know it sounds cold and harsh, but it's who I am or was. It took me a while but I slowly learned the importance of relationships. Then creating them became easier.

Paul's emphasis on relationships

Paul shows us the importance of relationships to spread his message. He met the community exactly where he found them: in their homes, with strong and weak faith, working-class and upper-class people, and complicated family situations. He learned their struggles, belief systems, and challenges. Paul says,

> *"To the Jews I became like a Jew, to win the Jews. To those under the law I became like one under the law (though I myself am not under the law), so as to win those under the law. To those not having the law I became like one not having the law (though I am not free from God's law but am under Christ's law), so as to win those not having the law. To the weak I became weak, to win the weak. I have become all things to all people so that by all possible means I might save some. I do all this for the sake of the gospel, that I may share in its blessings."* 1 Cor. 9:20-23

Paul empathized with all people and not just those he liked. This relationship-building technique provided him access into their situations and circumstances, which built trust and furthered his ministry.

"To the weak I became weak." To those low on the economic ladder, he became like them. He connected with the people he wanted to reach.

Making connections in leadership

Connections and relationships are the backbone of strong leadership. Paul shows us the importance of connections and building relationships the same way he learned through Jesus. Jesus says, *"Love your neighbor as yourself."* Mark 12:31

How do you love your neighbor or employee? The first step is to know them. Jesus tells us to truly love our neighbor. A relationship filled with encouragement and support.

Think about relationships with your employees and co-workers. How much do you know about them or their families? Where did they grow up? What do they like to do? Are they involved in community organizations? To love your neighbor or employees as yourself, you need to know them personally.

Sense of belonging

So why is this important?

Allen and Kern (2019) state "most people have a deep desire to connect with others. We long to feel valued and supported. We long to share our thoughts, emotions, and life with others."[1]

Knowing employees on a personal level creates a sense of belonging and builds trust. Most people want a sense of belonging in the workplace. A place where they feel part of a group and that promotes a culture of inclusion at all levels of the organization. Building a sense of belonging increases employee engagement which directly correlates to an increase in financial performance.

"Organizations with highly engaged employees experience increased customer satisfaction, profits and employee productivity."[2] This is the bottom line of why creating a sense of belonging is important to the organization's future.

A sense of belonging at the workplace is the same feeling you feel when belonging to a club.

At eight years old, my Brownie troop went to summer camp. The feeling of "being with the girls" brought warmth and love through fun and laughter. We huddled under blankets and held the flashlight under our chin and told ghost stories late into the night. Finally, the troop leader said, "Girls! Shhhh!" Giggling, we went to sleep. I was part of a club. I belonged.

> Think about your experiences where you felt a sense of belonging. How did you feel? Who was there? What type of club or group?

Social networks

Social networks are built-in in traditional offices. Co-workers become friends. Everyone's mission is the same when we belong to the same company, department, and team.

The connection and relationship with my co-worker/best friend are important to my sense of belonging. The ability to be together at lunch every day and chat about our families and challenges in our work life brings us closer together.

However, my social network instantly disappeared when I became an entrepreneur. Daily lunch-hour conversations didn't happen. The energy and connection created during lunch were missing. A sense of loneliness replaced the sense of belonging.

To minimize the loneliness and find the sense of belonging, it's important to intentionally create social experiences. To most of us, friends are an important piece of our lives. Personal conversations, joking, laughing, and solving problems give energy.

Do you remember a time when your life was (possibly) turned upside down overnight? One day you're laughing and sharing with colleagues, and the next you're in a basement cubicle at the computer trying to figure out how to work from home.

This is what happened to most people in March 2020 when COVID-19 hit the U.S. If you worked from home during the pandemic, the sense of loneliness may have replaced the sense of belonging.

> **TIP:** Be intentional with your friends and network. Schedule time on your calendar to connect and build relationships. This prevents the sense of loneliness from slowly replacing the sense of belonging. This is especially true in remote work situations.

Creating a sense of belonging in the workplace

The "human side" of the boss

Why is it important for the boss to bring their human side to work? Most employees want the boss to open up and bring their whole self to work. Their professional and personal lives. When professional and personal lives are separated, life becomes full of exhaustion and isolation. The isolation creates barriers between employees and the boss which reduces communication and creates a hierarchy difficult to remove.

They say it's lonely at the top, and that is true but it doesn't have to be. Bringing my whole-self to work was difficult and against my personality. And it created barriers between me and the employees with each promotion.

Isolation.

Intentionally, connecting with employees on a personal level created a safe environment to openly share feedback and increase engagement. It created cohesiveness and the sense of belonging I didn't realize was missing.

Opening up and being the boss

Is there a balance between opening up and being the boss? It depends. The more you open up and let the employees know you on a personal level, the closer the connection becomes. Employees know you're the boss. Letting them into your personal life doesn't reduce your authority, but it does help them know your story.

> **TIP:** Find a natural time to open up to the team, i.e., before a meeting or in the coffee room.
> Going into a department unannounced and asking personal questions may make the employee(s) uneasy. They may question your motives regardless of your words.

Ask questions

Spending time and connecting with your staff and co-workers is one way to create a sense of belonging. Most people connect to those who are similar. Employees connect to other employees in the same way.

But it goes deeper than that. I'm talking about creating a *culture* of belonging for everyone. "For many, work becomes an important source of belonging with others, through shared interests with colleagues, a sense of purpose found in one's work, and providing social interactions with others."[3]

Intentionally connecting to your employees and co-workers is the first step. Uncover their passions, interests, and hobbies. If an employee has a passion for photography, show interest in their work or ask for advice on what camera to purchase.

The conversation produces a feeling of value and shows that you're interested in who they are and not just their productivity.

Ideas to create a sense of belonging culture

Everyone has to eat. Having lunch with one another is a perfect way to let your guard down and get to know each other. It removes perceived barriers between the boss and employees and builds trust.

Cater lunch or, to make it fun, organize a potluck lunch where everyone brings a dish to pass. Have a contest where everyone brings their favorite dish and votes for the best dessert or chili. This brings a sense of camaraderie and belonging.

Why not turn it into a fundraising event for a local charity? This takes it to a deeper level when giving is involved. What about arranging a holiday party and everyone brings a dish to pass?

Here's a fun holiday party idea:

'TWAS THE NIGHT BEFORE CHRISTMAS WHITE ELEPHANT POTLUCK PARTY

- Each person brings their favorite main dish, dessert, or snack.
- Each person brings a white elephant gift. A white elephant gift is something that you no longer want and want to re-gift.
- Have each person put the wrapped gift on the gift table.
- After lunch, each person takes the gift they brought and puts it in front of them. Arrange the tables in a circle.
- Select someone to read the book *'Twas the Night Before Christmas*.
- Each time the reader says the word "and," pass the gift to the person on your right.
- When the story is finished, the gift in front of you is the one you open (as long as it is not your own).
- Take turns opening the gifts so everyone shares in the laughter.

A friend and co-worker introduced our team to the party idea. It's great fun and a wonderful way to create memories that bring the team closer together. Incorporate it into your family Christmas traditions as well. So much fun, and it removes the stress of gift buying.

Team-building events

Another way to create a sense of belonging and camaraderie is through team-building events. At your next special meeting or event, schedule time on the agenda for team-building.

If possible, use a third-party company to organize the event, which reduces stress on the meeting organizer. Third-party team-building organizations have proven team-building ideas which increase success rates.

Shhhh...The secret is to schedule it. It won't happen naturally.

The power of surveys

Surveys are a great way to identify team activities. Some team members may not be comfortable giving feedback face-to-face, so an anonymous survey works best to get honest answers.

SAMPLE SURVEY QUESTIONS

Include an introduction to explain the reason for the survey and how the feedback will be used.

1. On a scale of 1 – 5, what is the likelihood you'd attend a team-building event?
   a. 1 = will not attend, 2 = not likely, 3 = maybe, it depends on the event, 4 = likely, and 5 = absolutely
   a. If rated a 3 or below, provide comments as to why.
2. Choose one of the following options for a team-building event. (Include options that fit your budget and location.) Be sure to include an "other" option to allow the employee to enter their own ideas.
3. Choose one of the following dates and times for the event.
4. Provide additional comments.
5. Send a satisfaction survey following the event. This provides feedback on the success rate and suggested changes for the next event.

Retreats

Retreats incorporate team building with business. Schedule an annual retreat during the business-planning process.

Rather than going to a hotel, rent a large vacation home where everyone has their own room and bathroom. It's still private but yet forces the team to interact in the kitchen and common living areas.

Have a karaoke party and assign teams to make dinner each night. Business is conducted in a casual atmosphere during the day, and relationships are built in the evenings around dinner, drinks, and games.

The Intersection between skills, background, & jobs

Have there been times when home situations drifted into your work relationships or performance?

A sick child or parent.

A fight with your spouse or partner that stays with you throughout the day.

Most companies ask employees to work more, which blurs the lines between personal and professional lives. Bringing your "whole self" to work develops a sense of belonging while creating stronger connections and builds a trust-filled environment.

Employee's skills connect to their background

Typically, people gravitate toward jobs they are good at and enjoy. I realize not everyone has the opportunity to enjoy their work. But most people seek careers they enjoy.

The job training and career counseling industry is estimated at $16bn in 2020[4]. It is estimated to grow 8% between 2019 and 2029.[5]

The large market size and estimated growth rate shows us that people seek jobs they like and are good at.

My career began shipping equipment to South America because I spoke Spanish, which I enjoyed. I applied for the bilingual documents clerk position because I wanted to speak Spanish, and not because the shipping industry was my passion. Speaking Spanish was the top priority.

The truth is that I majored in Spanish because I loved to talk, and if I spoke another language, I could talk to so many more people.

After all, I was voted most talkative in high school.

The Spanish culture was where I belonged. My career aligned with what I loved and the skills I had.

If we were having coffee right now, I'd ask your story and how you found your job. Why did you choose your career?

Send me an e-mail and share your story.

Jobs shape employees

The employee's experience in the work environment shapes who they are. Jobs shape people as they perform them, so management must care about the job's impact on the whole person.[6]

Knowledge gained, leadership skills acquired, empowerment, sense of belonging, and management's leadership style play a part in shaping a person.

Why is this important to recognize?

Well, the employee's workplace atmosphere can spill into their personal life.

Work environments filled with political games and stress may negatively impact the employee's personal life.

But a positive culture may positively impact the employee's personal life when it's full of open communication, a team environment, advancement opportunities, and value.

A positive workplace environment can not only impact the employee but also their family.

Management's role

As a manager, what can you do about it? Focus and be intentional on the job's impact on the whole person.

- How do the actual work tasks impact the employee?
- How does the environment impact the employee?
- How does the team dynamics impact the employee?
- How do the relationships between the employees impact the employee?

Answers to these questions uncover how the company, department, and culture impact the employee's personal and professional lives or whole self.

The jobs I performed and the leaders I had shaped my leadership style and approach.

Proper etiquette, customer service levels, positive business decisions, strong business ethics, and creating a culture of high expectations are examples of skills and attributes I learned from my jobs, bosses, and company culture.

Leaders and managers

Strong leaders positively shape employees' opinions of the company, its leadership, and overall work experience, and weak managers negatively shape employees' opinions and work experience.

Strong leader

A strong leader empowers others, communicates freely, actively listens to understand, and creates a sense of belonging.

Weak manager

A weak manager supervises the workforce. Typically, their top priority is completing tasks. Many feel that employee development is the responsibility of the employee.

Leadership assessment

Complete the leadership assessment on the next page to identify leadership attributes to incorporate into your leadership style to become a *strong or stronger* leader.

Reference the sample assessment after the instructions to clarify any questions.

LEADER ASSESSMENT ACTIVITY:

Download the Leader Assessment Activity template from www.graceandsaltbook.com under the resources tab.

The Leader Assessment Activity template has two columns: Strong Leaders on the left and Weak Managers on the right side.

Instructions to complete the assessment:

STEP 1. Under the Strong Leaders column write down the names of three leaders you consider strong leaders. Leaders you want to emulate.

STEP 2. Below the column heading write leadership characteristics they demonstrate. How do or did they make you feel when you're (were) around them? Do (did) you want to please them and do the absolute best job ever? Consider why you feel that way. What did they do?

STEP 3. Under the column Weak Managers, write down three names you consider weak managers. Think about people you consider poor leaders. How do (did) they make you feel? What characteristics do (did) they have?

STEP 4. Compare the two columns. Who do you want to work for?

STEP 5. Now, think about your own leadership style.

STEP 6. Choose two strong leader characteristics to incorporate into your leadership style.

STEP 7. Write a plan to reach this goal. Reference the Activity Sample below.

LEADERSHIP ASSESSMENT ACTIVITY (SAMPLE)

STRONG LEADERS	WEAK MANAGERS
John Smith	Ken McNally
Jane Doe	Susy Smith
Katie Owens	Bob Perfect

CHARACTERISTICS

STRONG LEADERS	WEAK LEADERS
(Clear & Consistent Communication)	Micro-Managing
Development	No Communication
(Sense of Belonging)	Intimidating

CHARACTERISTICS

CHARACTERISTIC	ACTION	TIMELINE
Clear & Consistent Communication	1. Advise team of plan to improve communication. 2. Send anonymous survey to team on my communication style & effectiveness. 3. Evaluate feedback. 4. Incorporate feedback into plan. 5. Establish communication council (2-3 trusted colleagues) to provide accountability, input, and progress. 6. Follow-up survey with team members on progress.	1. January 15 2. January 20 3. By February 28 4. By March 30 5. By March 30 6. October 31
Sense of Belonging	1. Advise team of plan to incorporate sense of belonging into culture. 2. Send anonymous survey to team on sense of belonging and their thoughts on how to create this culture. 3. Evaluate feedback. 4. Incorporate feedback into plan. 5. Establish sense of belonging council (2-3 trusted colleagues) to provide accountability, input, and progress. 6. Follow-up survey with team members on progress.	1. January 15 2. January 20 3. By February 28 4. By March 30 5. By March 30 6. October 31

The plan includes the characteristic you want to develop, actions, and completion dates.

Communication & sense of belonging councils

In the plan, I've included communication and sense of belonging councils. The councils' purpose is accountability, plan adjustment, and measurement. The council creates a two-way communication method that ensures leadership communication disseminates throughout the organization and that feedback from the workforce reaches leadership's ears. The council members must be trusted by both leadership and the workforce. Don't filter the workforce's feedback. Honest communication is critical to create a sense of belonging.

Share all objectives and timelines at one time with the workforce. It may be too much information to absorb, but it's important the employees know the entire plan rather than sharing additional objectives at a later date. Transparency is critical no matter the message.

Great leaders

Great leaders make employees feel valued by listening to the employee's thoughts and opinions. They are direct when performance isn't meeting expectations and lead the discussions with grace & salt. They pull high-performing employees up through the organization, teaching leadership lessons along the way.

Building a sense of belonging opens the door for employees to bring their whole self to work. It's at this point where the employee gravitates toward what they enjoy and are good at. If the employee loves what they do, the experience positively impacts both their professional and personal lives.

Lesson II: Build an environment filled with a sense of belonging and trust through Paul's method of connecting with one another.

To the weak I became weak, to win the weak. I have become all things to all people so that by all possible means I might save some. 1 Corinthians 9:22

GREAT LEADERSHIP ATTRIBUTES EXAMPLE

These are attributes demonstrated by one of my mentors.

- Built relationships based on trust.
- Questioned the status quo.
- Challenged processes.
- Listened to understand.
- Cared for the employees.
- Put the organization and customers above himself.
- High expectations and communicated those expectations.
- High integrity.

He shaped me and my leadership style. And exemplifies Grace & Salt leadership.

LESSON III: SERVING & GIVING

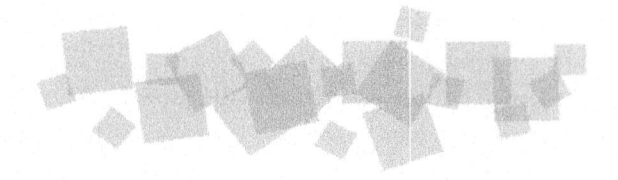

*For even the Son of Man did not come to be served,
but to serve, and to give his life as ransom for many.*
Mark 10:45

It's a typical November day. The cold wind kisses my face as I sway back and forth on the front porch swing. The red-checked flannel blanket is warm and cozy as I silently reminisce about the leaders that have come and gone in my life. How many showed a servant heart or led with servant leadership?

Serving others

Many Jesus scholars consider His leadership style as servant leadership. The term servant leadership was originally introduced in 1970 by Robert K. Greenleaf.[1] Greenleaf defined servant leadership as:

> The servant-leader is servant first… It begins with the natural feeling that one wants to serve, to serve first. Then conscious choice brings one to aspire to lead. That person is sharply different from one who is leader first.

The leader-first and the servant-first are two extreme types. Between them there are shadings and blends that are part of the infinite variety of human nature.

The difference manifests itself in the care taken by the servant-first to make sure that other people's highest priority needs are being served.

The best test, and difficult to administer, is: Do those served grow as persons? Do they, while being served, become healthier, wiser, freer, more autonomous, more likely themselves to become servants? And, what is the effect on the least privileged in society? Will they benefit or at least not be further deprived?

A servant-leader focuses primarily on the growth and well-being of people and the communities to which they belong. The servant-leader shares power, puts the needs of others first and helps people develop and perform as highly as possible. (para. 1-4)

Greenleaf's statement of "it begins with a natural feeling that one wants to serve" is the foundation for a servant-leader.

Jesus and Greenleaf's Best Test

Let's take a look at Jesus and His leadership style. Is Jesus a servant leader? We'll use Greenleaf's Best Test to evaluate Jesus's leadership style.

Greenleaf's Best Test Question One

1. Did those Jesus served grow as persons?

Paul served Jesus. Did he grow as a person?

We'll review a simplified and paraphrased version of Paul's background to provide context to Paul's (Saul's) story.

Paul's Story

Paul's original name was Saul, and he was a Pharisee (an authority of

Jewish law). As Saul, he persecuted Jewish people who believed in Jesus Christ.

"...Saul was still breathing out murderous threats against the Lord's disciples." Acts 9:1

"...if he found any there who belonged to the Way, whether men or women, he might take them as prisoners to Jerusalem." Acts 9:2

On his way to Damascus to identify followers of Jesus and jail them, he was blinded by a bright light and received a message from Jesus. Jesus told him to go into Damascus, and he would be given directions.

Saul opened his eyes and he was blind. The men traveling with him held his hand the rest of the way to Damascus. Upon arrival, he prayed and fasted for three days.

God instructed Ananias to go to Saul and pray over him. Ananias knew Saul's reputation of persecuting Jesus followers but followed the Lord's instructions anyway.

Following Ananias's prayer, Saul opened his eyes and he could see. After getting baptized and gaining his strength, he followed the Lord's instructions and traveled to Damascus to preach that Jesus is Lord.

Greenleaf's Best Test Question Two

> *2. Did Paul (Saul) become healthier, wiser, freer, more autonomous, and more likely themselves to become servants under Jesus's leadership?*

Saul is referred to as Paul in Acts 13. A complete transformation. Paul's life changed through his interactions with Jesus, and he dedicated his life to spread Christianity. Paul is credited for the expansion of the Christian faith and wrote or was the main focus in thirteen out of twenty-seven books in the New Testament.

Greenleaf's Best Test Question Three

> *3. What was the impact on the least privileged in society under Jesus's leadership, and did they benefit from His leadership?*

Jesus's philosophy is summed up in the following verses.

"Blessed are the meek, for they will inherit the earth." Matthew 5:5

"...for whoever exalts themselves will be humbled, and whoever humbles themselves will be exalted." Matthew 23:12

Jesus's leadership tells us to clothe those who need clothes and feed those who are hungry and thirsty. If we follow Jesus's teachings, the least privileged benefit greatly.

Use Greenleaf's Best Test to identify servant leaders and leadership in your organization.

GREENLEAF'S BEST TEST QUESTIONS

1. Do those served grow as persons?
2. Do they, while being served, become healthier, wiser, freer, more autonomous, more likely themselves to become servants?
3. What is the effect on the least privileged in society? Will they benefit or at least not be further deprived?

If the answers to these questions are yes, then the leader is a servant leader.

How to create a servant's heart

Creating a servant's heart is the first step in transitioning to a servant leader. If serving others isn't natural for you or you haven't discovered it yet, it's critical to be intentional in serving. It takes from 18 to 254 days to change a behavior.[2]

The following tips create the behavior of a servant heart.

8 TIPS TO CREATE A SERVANT'S HEART

1. Set a goal to participate in _____ number of serving events in the next 6 months.
2. Schedule time in your calendar to research events. A calendar is the perfect tool to track your goals.
3. Focus on events that interest you. Don't participate in serving events that don't bring you joy. A servant heart is strongest when connected to the cause.
4. Tell your family and team of the goal and ask them to keep you accountable.
5. Invite family, friends, and co-workers to join. Creating special memories is a great way to serve.
6. After each event, publish a short article about the event, its purpose, and the outcome. This promotes the event and encourages others to follow your example.
7. Track your progress toward your goal and adjust your goal as necessary.
8. Ask others what serving opportunities they have and if you can join them.

Before continuing with the study of servant leadership, it's important to understand the types of power and how to identify Teflon and ego leadership styles. I'll define these leadership styles shortly.

Power and influence

Personal, legitimate, and expert power are three types of power leaders' exhibit.

Personal power

A charismatic leader has personal power—the ability to gain followers.

When you think about charisma, what traits come to mind? Perhaps you think of someone who is charming, magnetic, and confident. John F.

Kennedy, Jimmy Fallon, Will Smith, Ellen DeGeneres, and Oprah Winfrey all have personal power.

On a personal level, you may know a charismatic person in your company, church, or family. The person who has a presence but can't describe it.

They may be passionate about a cause or a goal and engage others in the mission. Following them is easy, and their charismatic personal power leads others to their causes.

Examples of causes may be challenging the country to put a man on the moon or simply influencing others to follow their initiative. Charisma is powerful when used for good or evil.

Legitimate power

Legitimate power is held by someone with influence because of their position. The president of your organization or the chairperson of a committee are examples of leaders with legitimate power. If you're the boss, you have legitimate power. You give directives for others to follow.

Expert power

Expert power is a specialist with specific knowledge.

A surgeon has expert power because they have education and training in their specific area of study. An employee who knows features and benefits of the equipment and how they impact the customer has expert power.

An example would be a technical trainer. They would have expert power because they know how to fix equipment and transfer their knowledge to service technicians through training sessions.

The Art of Teflon

In 1938, Dr Roy J. Plunkett accidentally discovered polytetrafluoroethylene or Teflon. This substance is considered the "most slippery material in existence."[3]

In leadership, we encounter some leaders who are the most slippery people in existence.

They have mastered the art of Teflon. They disappear during a difficult situation or sidestep their involvement to avoid responsibility.

HOW TO IDENTIFY TEFLON LEADERS

Use this checklist to identify Teflon leaders.

- Their words and actions don't align. They say one thing but do another.
- They take credit for successes and are out of sight for failures.
- They appear authentic and caring, but their motive is self-serving.
- They are full of ideas but delegate the work to others.
- At first, you believe their words but soon your instincts tell you something is wrong.
- You begin to avoid them and only interact if told to.

Ego Leadership

One challenge in leadership is removing our ego.

Ego is a part of confidence that is required in decision-making, networking, and interpersonal relationships. The key is not to let ego drive decisions or behaviors.

When it does, I refer to it as Ego Leadership.

Do you know someone who leads with their ego?

They may have legitimate power (boss), expert power (specialist), or personal power (charisma).

How do they make decisions? Are they self-rewarding?

Are they Teflon?

Dealing with Ego Leadership

Although dealing with ego leadership may be challenging and frustrating, it's these experiences that shape your own leadership style.
So how do you deal with ego leadership?

HOW TO DEAL WITH EGO LEADERSHIP

If you find yourself with a leader who demonstrates ego leadership, ask yourself these questions:

1. Do you work for or with a leader who demonstrates an ego leadership style?
2. Are you happy in the organization?
3. Do your values align with the organization's leadership and culture?

- If you answered yes, to the above questions, then *trust* yourself and know that these leaders come and most go, especially if their actions are contrary to the organization's culture.
- If your ethics and morals aren't jeopardized, *deal* with them. They will probably move to another role or leave the organization.
- *Focus* on the company and customers and forget the drama that ego leadership may create.

Ego leadership doesn't typically survive in a non-ego culture. Either the person adapts or they leave the organization.

Servant Leadership

Jesus taught us to be servants to others, to put others first, and to teach.

Mark 9:35 says, *"Sitting down, Jesus called the Twelve and said, 'Anyone who wants to be first must be the very last, and the servant of all.'"*

In Galatians 5:13, it says, *"You, my brothers and sisters, were called to be* free. But do not use your freedom to indulge the flesh; rather, <u>serve one another humbly in love.</u>"

In John 13:14-17, after washing the disciples' feet, He said, *"Now that I, your Lord and Teacher, have washed your feet, you also should wash one another's feet. I have set you an example that <u>you should do as I have done for you.</u> Very truly I tell you, <u>no servant is greater than his master,</u> nor is a messenger greater than the one who sent him. Now that you know these things, you will be blessed if you do them."*

It's time to incorporate the servant leadership philosophy to your existing style.

How to transition to a servant leader

The best way to transition to a servant leader is to talk to your employees. Discuss their challenges and daily stresses. If asking these questions to your team is new, then explain your intentions first or the employees may become suspicious.

At first, the discussion may be awkward and forced. They may be uncomfortable sharing and admitting their challenges. Start where they want to start. Make connections, take it slow, and build trust.

Once they've shared a few challenges, think about how you could relieve that stress. The solution could be supporting their proposed changes and encouraging them to take action.

Many times, employees want to be heard and supported so *they* can make the necessary changes. To build a culture of accountability, the responsibility of taking action and making changes is up to the employees.

You might be thinking. "How can I remove *their* stress when *I* have so much on my plate? I don't want to make a promise I can't keep."

True; you don't want to make a false promise. The fact you asked tells them you care.

Competing priorities

Help them prioritize competing projects or competing requests from various bosses. Competing priorities overwhelm employees. After all, how many bosses do you have?

In most organizations, directions come from various department leaders. If the employee is lower in the organization, they receive directions from several leaders in addition to their direct supervisor. For some employees, this is overwhelming and intimidating.

- What happens if they say no to an assignment?
- What happens if they prioritize someone's request below another's?
- What happens if they ask clarifying questions to an executive? Most of the time, the employee needs support to navigate the requests and manage another boss's request.

SERVANT LEADERSHIP JOURNAL PROMPT

Take some time to journal using the below prompts.

- Think about when you worked in an entry-level position.
  Ask yourself, what challenges did I experience?
  How would I have felt if my boss asked me about my daily challenges and stress? What would I have told them?

- Based on the above answers, what questions will I ask my team members?
- Write down your plan to talk to your team. When is a good time? How will you begin? What questions will you ask? What location will it be at? (Conference room, your office or theirs?) Who will be there (everyone or one at a time)?

Preparation for the conversation is critical to open dialogue with the employees. Anticipate their thoughts, concerns, and questions. Communication should be a two-way street.

Serving & giving

Servant leadership includes both serving and giving. What's the difference?

Serving is <u>willingly</u> serving others before yourself. Offering help to someone before considering your own needs. Serving becomes second nature and is automatic.

Giving is <u>choosing</u> to give products and talents to others. To have a giving heart means you make a conscious choice to give.

Many times, serving and giving go hand-in-hand.

How to incorporate a giving mindset

"For I was hungry and you gave me something to eat, I was thirsty and you gave me something to drink, I was a stranger and you invited me in, I needed clothes and you clothed me, I was sick and you looked after me, I was in prison and you came to visit me." Matthew 25:35-36.

Would you consider yourself a giving person?

If so, incorporate one new giving activity into your schedule. If not, review the steps to incorporate a giving mindset into your life.

CREATING A GIVING MINDSET - GIVING MINDSET IDEAS

- Identify your special skills, talents, and resources.
- Write down local charities or organizations that align with your values. Choose organizations you're passionate about.
- Research social media for organizations that need donations.
- Contact local food pantries, homeless shelters, and churches for donation needs.
- Organize a food or clothing drive.
- Organize a fundraising event.
- Organize a blood drive.

To give time, talents, and resources to others is another way to serve and build a sense of belonging among your team. A fundraising drive to support the local food pantry brings the team together around a cause.

Letting God lead

In 2006, heading to West Virginia on our first mission trip, my goal was to create a closer relationship with God.

At that time in my life, the feeling of emptiness permeated my days, and I felt a pull to seek God. Sweating, praying, and spending time alone was the week's plan.

Two adults and two students from our church including me and my daughter, Amanda, attended the trip.

Upon arriving in West Virginia, we received our jobs for the week.

"Mom, let's teach Vacation Bible School together, okay?" Amanda asked.

Vacation Bible School? That isn't sweating and spending time alone with God.

"Of course, if you'd feel more comfortable," I said.

"Awesome. Thank you!"

Great. Interacting with screaming kids, scissors, and glue is not what I planned. Okay, God, take this week from me and do with it what You will. Let it be Your will and not mine.

God answered my prayer. The following day, a chaperone asked me to trade places with her. Her job site was too physical, and she wasn't able to help the team.

Hallelujah!

I asked Amanda if she was okay with the change in plans. She was. She had settled into the trip and was comfortable with her new friends.

Broken gravestones littered the old and forgotten cemetery. The sweat poured down my back as I maneuvered the sod-filled wheelbarrow up and down the hillside to the sunken grave sites.

Thank you, God. This work was physical and exactly what I needed.

Learning to let God lead was freeing. It provided freedom I had never felt.

This lesson taught me how to see His messages and direction and relax. I was not alone.

How to let God lead

If you're like me, you like to control every aspect of your life including your work life. Letting God lead is much easier and less stressful. Knowing that God is in control removes the stress of what to do next. He shows the way, but you have to accept it and follow it.

But how do you do that?

Constant and consistent prayer. Following are three steps to give God control.

HOW TO LET GOD LEAD

1. Pray. Ask God to take control. Tell Him you will let Him lead. Pray the same prayer every day and every time you feel yourself taking control.
2. Talk to God about His plans for your life. What does He want you to do and where does He want you to go? Ask Him specifically to show you the way.
3. Read the Bible. He will show you the way through His word.
4. Listen and be still. Rest your mind.
5. Pay attention. Being still in a busy, crazy world allows you to pay attention to God's messages and *messengers*. He sends instructions through others and by opening opportunities.

Turning a pandemic into a fundraising opportunity

The COVID-19 pandemic is a good example of finding opportunity to serve and give out of a bad situation. Most of the US workforce works from home, and businesses have closed temporarily, permanently, or have furloughed employees.

In March 2020, the Governor of Illinois, where I live, issued a shelter-in-place order that required everyone to stay home except for going to work, essential errands, or emergencies. By April, the US unemployment rate was 14%.

What could I do to help?

My schedule is more flexible than others and putting the community ahead of my business goals was top priority.

Cool. The local upholstery company is seeking volunteers to sew non-surgical face masks. I should make masks. I can sew (somewhat). This is it! My opportunity to help!

Jumping into my car, I arrive at the upholstery company and become a mask-maker.

Using Facebook to get the word out, I post that I've volunteered to make masks and ask my Facebook friends to join the cause.

Some friends join the mask-making mania and then others ask, "Hi Melissa. Are they for sale?"

Hmm...that's a great idea! I could turn my mask making into a fundraiser for the local homeless shelter. Let's raise funds for the Rockford Rescue Mission.

There's no time like the present. It's April 13th. I'll launch the event on the 15th.

NEED A MASK?
$10 EACH
PROCEEDS DONATED TO THE ROCKFORD RESCUE MISSION

Contact Melissa (Mackey) McCormick on Facebook
or email: masksbymel@gmail.com

Other prints available. Masks available while supplies last.

The program is announced, and friends with serving and giving hearts immediately contact me.

"Hi, Melissa. I have some fabric scraps you can use. I was going to make a quilt but never got around to it. Can you use extra fabric?"

"Thanks so much, Sue. Absolutely. I'll swing by this afternoon."

Masks by Mel is born. The orders trickle in and with little advertising, sales grow.

My goal is to make masks cool and fashionable. If we have to wear them, we should wear team colors, such as the Bears or Packers, or plaid, stripes, or Hawaiian flowers. But there's a problem. The fabric stores are closed so my fabric choices are limited.

The fabric I have isn't very masculine. What can I use for men? The fabric stores are closed. So... I know! I'll use Mike's shirts.

"Hey, Mike, I'm having trouble finding nice colors and fabric designs for men. Would it be okay if I used some of your shirts to make masks?"

"That's a good idea. I'll get some that would make cool masks."

In May, the local fabric store opens with curbside pick-up only which expands fabric design options.

And then, it happens...

"Hi, Melissa. I saw your Facebook post on the mask fundraising event. I'd like to interview you. Are you willing to set up an interview via Zoom?" a television reporter asks.

"Absolutely." *What? The local TV station wants to interview me and my fundraiser?*

The power of television. Orders are through the roof!

We raised over $1,600 ($1,608.85) in fifteen days. My daughter handled customer service activities, my husband purchased elastic and other supplies, and my mom helped sew. We established a small manufacturing business out of the basement overnight.

The reason this story is important is to give an example of how to give your talents to others in a time of need. The community rallied around the fundraising event to support the Rockford Rescue Mission.

My family rallied around the purpose and cause. We created a sense of belonging, gave our time, talents, and resources to others, and served the community.

Below are ideas on how to incorporate a giving mindset into your organization's culture.

WAYS TO INCORPORATE A GIVING MINDSET INTO THE CULTURE

1. Refer to the Giving Mindset ideas previously outlined.
2. Survey your team for giving ideas that they are passionate about.
3. Have your team choose one or two giving activities.
4. Assign the event leader and committee members. This builds engagement Rotate event leaders and committee members through the year.
5. Establish a budget for the event and communicate it to the team.
6. Promote the events on social media, including the company's page and the employee's personal pages, which also promotes the organization and its giving & serving culture.
7. Tell friends, family, and colleagues of the events to build a sense of belonging, loyalty, and pride of the organization.
8. Provide paid time to volunteer during work hours.
9. Invite families to join.
10. Build an environment and culture of giving by encouraging them to contribute to the community during work hours.
11. Post pictures of the events on social media.
12. Incorporate serving and giving events into the organization's business plan. This solidifies serving and giving into the culture of the organization.

Don't let the world and busy life consume your energy so that one day when you're exhausted, sitting on the couch, you'll say, "I wish I had done _____ to help _____."

Be intentional with incorporating serving and giving into your personal and professional lives. It increases your impact on the organization's culture, team, community, and yourself.

Lesson III: Choose to lead with a servant-heart and be a generous giver of your time, talents, & resources.

"For even the Son of Man did not come to be served, but to serve, and to give his life as ransom for many." Mark 10:45

LESSON IV: REMOVE INACTIVE YEAST SWIFTLY

...Don't you know that a little yeast leavens the whole batch of dough? Get rid of the old yeast, so that you may be a new unleavened batch—as you really are. For Christ, our Passover lamb, has been sacrificed. Therefore let us keep the Festival, not with the old bread leavened with malice and wickedness, but with the unleavened bread of sincerity and truth.
1 Corinthians 5:6-8

*A*ctive yeast is to bread as high-performing employees are to a growing company. Healthy, active yeast is the critical ingredient to make dough rise. Once it's old, the organisms are less active and die which means the dough takes longer to rise. [1]

The basic science behind yeast is active yeast is an organism that consumes sugars. Eating sugar creates a byproduct of carbon dioxide and alcohol. The byproduct causes the dough to rise. Inactive yeast creates the byproduct at lower levels.

Yeast and employee productivity

Applying Corinthians 5:6-8 to team productivity states that *"a little yeast leavens the whole batch of dough"* or active employees raise the productivity of the team. This analogy illustrates the inactive (old) yeast as the poor performing employee or an employee who isn't aligned with the vision, mission, or strategy of the organization.

"Get rid of the old yeast, so that you may be a new unleavened batch—as you really are." 1 Corinthians 5:7

Let's review the evaluation from Lesson II on strong and weak leaders. What characteristics or attributes did you identify under the strong leaders column and what attributes did you identify under the weak managers column? The list may include managers who didn't reassign or terminate employees quickly or at all.

Inactive vs active yeast

The inactive yeast (poor performing or unaligned employee) must be removed from the batch of dough (team or organization) quickly. Imagine yeast molecules in their tennis shoes chasing sugar molecules, eating them, and releasing air bubbles into the dough.

The active yeast molecules work together and are aligned as a team. Their sole purpose is to produce air bubbles to make the dough rise.

Now, imagine inactive yeast molecules that are tired and rundown. They are no longer aligned with the active yeast. They shuffle their feet and move toward the sugar molecules. Eating sugar molecules doesn't interest them. They have other ideas on how to make the dough rise that isn't aligned with the original mission of producing air bubbles.

Let's take this analogy and overlay it with your team. Think about the employees on your team.

- Are any of them less active and just going through the motions?
- Are they disruptive to the team due to their inactivity or lack of production?
- Are they meeting their objectives or is it difficult to get them to move?

One of the hardest acts of a leader is to determine when it's time to remove the inactive yeast (poor performing employee) from the batch of dough (team or organization). It's common for leaders to make excuses for the individual's performance. Money and time are spent on sending them to development seminars, but their performance doesn't improve. In fact, the employee may not engage in the seminar but is glad to be out of the office. Unfortunately, most managers accept poor performance.

Making excuses and accepting poor performance

There are several possible reasons why poor performance is accepted.

Perhaps the conversation may be difficult. The manager doesn't know where to begin or how to approach the topic. They're uncomfortable with delivering the message for fear of how the employee will respond.

Another possible reason might be that the organization has a hiring freeze and "one body" is better than "*no* body." It's common to accept poor performance since "at least some work is being done at some level."

Finally, it's possible the manager leads with more grace and they like the person. Their preference is to approach the poor performance through development programs and continual conversations rather than face reality that the person doesn't fit in the role or organization any longer.

The best course of action for both the employee and the organization is to admit when the employee has become inactive yeast and acknowledge it's time to remove them from the dough.

Inactive yeast slows business down

Underperforming employees slow business in several ways:

1. The team becomes frustrated that the employee's poor performance is allowed, therefore, the team's productivity suffers.
2. The underperforming employee is disengaged and begins to perform poorly.
3. They may apply for a different position within the company or leave the company altogether.
4. Business slows down if an employee isn't aligned with the mission. They may not complete tasks or projects timely. They tell you they will complete the task, but they bury it in their inbox. This causes disruption to the department dynamics and decreases productivity while the other employees watch how the manager responds.

Active or inactive employees

Let's evaluate your team and determine who is active yeast (employees aligned with the organization's mission) and who is inactive or old yeast (employees not aligned with the organization's mission).

Download the Active or Inactive Employee Evaluation at www.graceandsaltbook.com/resources.

After completing the Active or Inactive Employee Evaluation document, answer the following questions.

- How many misaligned employees are there?
- What are the reasons they are misaligned?
- Are there hidden reasons for the poor performance?

If they truly are not aligned with the department's goals and have become misaligned or unwilling to carry out the company's vision, it's time to remove them from the team.

Inactive yeast scenario

While I'm sitting at my desk pouring through tons of shipping paperwork, the phone rings. Frantic, I dig through the mountain of papers to find the phone before the call goes to voicemail, and I answer it in a rush.

"Hello!"

"Hi, this is Jamie from ABC Logistics. I have a shipment for Sweden that has incorrect paperwork."

Again?

"Okay, thanks, I'll have the corrected invoice faxed over right away. Thanks for calling."

I've waited too long. I've known for years this wouldn't work out, but I thought maybe their work would improve. Do I really have to call human resources? They're such a nice person and I've never fired anyone.

"Documentation is critical," the human resources director says. "Be sure to document the discussion and send a copy for their file. Include a performance improvement plan in the discussion that will be monitored monthly. If the performance doesn't improve, we'll discuss next steps."

The challenge is that I've accepted their performance for five years. Why did I allow this performance level to continue? What prevented me from having discussions on their performance and the consequences if performance wasn't improved?

This scenario is from personal experience. Can you relate to this situation? The employee is pleasant, gentle, and gets along with the team. You've tried everything to improve their performance and, perhaps, complete some of their work.

Finally, the dreaded day comes. It's time to let them go. It would have been difficult even if they were the worst person in the world, but firing a nice, caring person makes matters worse. Letting employees go is one of the most difficult responsibilities for a supervisor and for an employee.

Scenario continues

My heart feels like it will break out of my chest, and my hands are dripping with sweat. Red splotches appear on my arms and neck, one by one until it looks like a sunburn.

It's time. I call the employee to my office. They enter the office and you can feel the tension in the air. I imagine they know this isn't going to be good. The human resources director gave me a choice to have the discussion in my office or in their office. I thought it best to have the discussion alone in my office.

The performance improvement plan is on my desk. We review the plan and the expectations one more time, and I can see the dread on their face. My guess is they've known for a while that this day would come but didn't know when. I stumble over my words with shaking hands and sweating palms. They say, "It's okay. I know I'm being fired."

We clean their desk and walk to their car. After a few long, deep breaths, I walk back to the office and explain to the team what happened. The team willingly worked additional hours to be sure our customer service level remained high.

Thinking back on it, I heard a sigh of relief from the team when it was over. Everyone knew the employee disrupted the team. The mistakes created more work. It was better to not have anyone in that position and work additional hours than to correct mistakes. This experience brought our team together with the same goals and objectives and created a strong sense of belonging and team connection.

Blessing in disguise

Later, I learned that the employee accepted a position at another organization where they thrived. A position that aligned with their skills and passion.

Lesson learned – preventing the future

Waiting years to act prevented the employee from finding the position that aligned with their values and skills. Many times, the employee knows it's not the right position or the right company but is reluctant to find a new job because of financial security, friendships, or fear.

I prevented their future by waiting five years to act.

Change your mindset when in this situation. Letting someone go is tough, but many times it's best for the employee and they are free to find their true purpose.

> Does this example resonate with you? What would you have done and how would you incorporate *Grace & Salt* into the discussions and the decision?
>
> Take a few moments to think about a situation where you're currently waiting to act.

The impact of delays

What is the impact of delaying the removal of the inactive yeast (poor performing employees) on other employees? When poor performance is accepted, high-performing employees get frustrated, and their engagement reduces.

Isn't it frustrating when special projects and additional work are given to you rather than your co-workers? On one hand, it's flattering that you're considered a good employee who is trusted and can handle extra work.

On the other hand, it's frustrating that your co-workers aren't given additional work to even out the workload. They leave the office on schedule and take breaks. The supervisor's inaction or indifference leads to a feeling that you're being taken for granted.

The go-to person

Once I became a supervisor, I realized it's easy to fall into the rhythm of giving special projects or added workload to the best employees or your "go-to" employees. The "go-to" employees are given special work or rush assignments because they are trusted and dependable. They understand the expectations, know how the boss thinks, and are strong communicators.

The downside to a "go-to" leadership style

When a leader continually relies on their "go-to" employee, employee engagement for other high-performing employees may diminish. Is another employee's poor performance the reason special projects are assigned to the high performers or "go-to" employees? If so, the team suffers when the poor performance is accepted.

Giving additional work or special assignments to "go-to" employees should be based on career advancement plans and not because their colleagues are poor performers.

Assigning projects to "go-to" employees

Who on your team are "go-to" employees? How do you assign special projects or assignments?

Be intentional about distributing special assignments to more than one team member. It's possible the poor or underperforming employee is disengaged. Giving special attention and assignments to other team members may engage the underperformer, and they may start to perform at a higher level.

To be successful with this strategy, strong communication is required. Be sure to communicate the expectations of the project, level of quality, and how often status updates are required.

Extending trust to an underperforming employee is risky but may be rewarding if or when they meet the expectations.

Definition of underperforming employees

There are two types of under-performing employees. The first is the employee who makes mistakes, misses deadlines, and doesn't improve after training and assistance.

The other type is the employee who isn't aligned with the organization's or supervisor's mission or vision. The employee prioritizes projects or their work schedule based on their goals and not the supervisor's. This delays the supervisor's projects and business slows down.

Unaligned employee scenario

Imagine an employee with expert power. Everyone seeks their advice, knowledge, and direction regarding the product line. They are the parts manager and *the* expert on everything parts and so much more. Part numbers, obsolete equipment, or knowing who to contact in the organization are reasons to call the parts manager.

Their influence goes far and wide. Their responsibility includes managing inventory levels, on-time delivery metrics, ensuring accurate shipments, and maintaining the high level of customer satisfaction.

Whew! First day after Christmas break. It's nice to be back, and the office is full of excitement for the new year. Well, let's see what's waiting in my inbox.

> To: Jack Hamilton, Parts Manager
> From: Sue Olson, Operations Supervisor
> Subject: SKU Streamline Project
> Dear Jack:
> I hope you had an enjoyable holiday break and are ready to start the new year with a mission-critical initiative. We'll be focused on streamlining our SKUs this year. The corporate office has instructed us to reduce the SKUs by 20% before the end of the first quarter. With this aggressive metric and quick turnaround, we'll need to begin the project immediately. Let's get together later today to discuss the plan.
> Thank you,
> Sue

"Hi, Sue. It's Jack. I just read your e-mail. Are you available now?"

"Sure, come on down. Thanks for jumping on this so quickly." *Well, sounds like he's on board with the plan.*

Jack and Sue sit down and establish their strategy. Jack will lead the initiative and begin identifying SKUs that haven't been sold in the past three years. He's agreed to send weekly updates to Sue.

Several weeks pass and Sue notices Jack's decisions aren't aligned with their original plan and progress has slowed considerably. Sue doesn't act on her concerns.

This isn't the first time that Jack's delayed projects, thinks Sue. *If I push him, will he leave the company? What will happen then? He's a valued employee with tons of knowledge.*

In this scenario, Jack is inactive yeast and slows business down. The SKU reduction initiative deadlines aren't met, and Sue doesn't hold Jack accountable. Sue's aware of the misalignment, but Jack originally appeared to agree with the initiative. He agreed and accepted the responsibility and the metrics. However, he prioritized other projects ahead of the SKU initiative.

It's time for Sue to address Jack's behavior and determine if Jack is more of a hinderance to the organization than a benefit.

Jack's expert power is so strong that the organization, including the executive team, is afraid of the ramifications if Jack were let go. How would the gap be filled?

Unaligned employee scenario continues

Sue's nervous and scared of what life would look like without Jack. After all, in many ways, Jack makes life easier. She doesn't worry about the parts business. He moves things along as he should but there is one *big* issue. He continues to delay her initiatives. She reflects on his past behavior. He never says he doesn't agree with her directives, but his actions state differently. How long will she let this go on? She knows that the more time passes, the harder it will be. After all, it's already been twenty years. Isn't it time to act? Will Sue be the one to make the difficult decision?

Then, she asks two critical questions.
"What will happen if I remove Jack?"
"What will happen if I *don't?*"

Ramifications if underperforming employees aren't removed swiftly

Although Jack has expert power and there may be a gap if he leaves, it's important to also consider the impact on the rest of the department. Nonaction demonstrates to other employees that Jack's behavior is acceptable.

They may exhibit similar behavior or begin to accept Jack's department mission rather than Sue's.

The other ramification is to the overall business. The business slows down because of Jack's nonverbal refusal to execute the plan. In today's environment or any environment, a business cannot afford to slow down.

Sue's decision

Sue knows that it's time to take action, develop the courage, and make the decision.

She contacts human resources, establishes a plan, and after following the appropriate human resources requirements (documentation, employee discussions, etc.), Jack is removed from the organization.

Sue reflects on the decision and outcome. *Boy, that was tough but I'm relieved. And you know, nothing happened. We didn't skip a beat. We didn't go out of business, and customers didn't cancel orders. Sure, there were times when it would have been easier to have Jack on the team. But it would have been a constant battle, which might have impacted the team or the company's goals might have been delayed or, worse, never achieved.*

The point

This example illustrates how even those employees that are seen as *"the expert"* can use their power against the company's goals. Their influence may derail the best strategy. Remember, the other employees are watching. The best course of action is to remove the underperforming employee as quickly as possible and not to succumb to the perception that the organization will falter without them.

Power matrix

Let's turn the discussion toward you and your experience. The power matrix analyzes the types of power from lesson III and applies them to your team. The analysis evaluates your direct employees and identifies their power type: expert, legitimate, or personal power. If you don't have direct employees, complete the power matrix personally.

Remove any bias you may have, positive or negative, toward the employee. I had a bias toward my star direct employee. (In that sentence, you see that I'm biased. I called her my "star" employee.) She was awesome and continually reinvented herself. However, when I evaluated her performance or growth potential, I removed the positive bias to objectively evaluate her performance. This wasn't easy to do, but I achieved my goal most of the time.

TIPS FOR A SUCCESSFUL POWER MATRIX.

- Dedicate time to complete the power matrix. Multiple sessions may be required. Typically, the answer isn't readily visible.
- If you aren't sure about an employee's power type, observe the employee.
- Be objective in your analysis and observations.
- Review the examples provided in the sample power matrix to help with the team or personal evaluation.

POWER MATRIX ACTIVITY

Review the questions and think through your responses.
If you don't have direct employees, complete the power matrix personally.
Download a copy of the sample power matrix at www.graceandsaltbook.com under the resources tab.

1. Determine power type by employee: personal, legitimate, or expert.
2. Do they use their influence and power for the good of the organization? Do they put the success of the organization above their own personal success? Are their motives purely to help customers and grow the business?
3. Are they aligned with the company's vision or your vision? If not, ask why. Has the vision been communicated? Do they understand it? Do they agree with it? Once you understand the reason(s) behind why they aren't aligned [listen to understand, first], put plans in place to resolve the situation.
4. Determine if the employees are in the right position. They are right for the company, but maybe they would provide more value in another role.
5. Determine the next steps. Identify actions that directly impact the organization's and department's goals. Examples are: role change, communicate the company vision in terms that the employees understand, or create a performance improvement plan.
6. Implement, execute, hold yourself accountable, and review annually.

As you brainstorm, add more thoughts into your analysis. This list of questions is to get you started.

EMPLOYEE POWER MATRIX (SAMPLE)

Sample Power Matrix	Type of Power: Expert or Personal	Influence Use: Organization or Personal	Aligned with leadership? Why or why not?	Right Position?	Next Steps
Employee A	Expert Power – Product Knowledge "Go-To" person.	Customer focused. Uses influence for organizational gain.	Aligned with leadership. Works to carry out organization's goals.	No. Value better served in a different role. (Elaborate on role & plan to move the employee.)	Determine new role, plan, and timing. Discuss with employee collaboratively.
Employee B	Personal Power – well known in company. Understands office politics.	Personal focused. Uses influence to advance career or influence.	Not aligned. Doesn't prioritize work with the org's goals. Not sure employee understands org's goals.	Yes, in right position.	Determine the reason the employee is not aligned. Implement improvement program for alignment and performance improvement.
Employee C	Legitimate Power – supervisor of the department.	Personal focused. Uses power to push own agenda.	Not aligned with leadership. Focused on personal career advancement.	Possibly. Need to discuss leadership style.	Discuss performance improvement plan. Consider supervisory training modules.

Each matrix is specific to each employee and situation. Once the power matrix is complete, it provides:

1. The type of power of each employee
2. How they use the power (for good or evil) and if it is used for the greater good of the organization
3. Alignment with the organization's and department's visions, and
4. Any required role changes.

THE BEST SOLUTION FOR REMOVING INACTIVE YEAST IS TO ONLY KEEP ACTIVE YEAST ON YOUR TEAM.

Lesson IV: Remove inactive yeast (underperforming employees) swiftly, which positively impacts the team and organization. Evaluate employee power types and determine if they use their power for personal gain or in the best interest of the company. Communicate with Grace & Salt.

...Don't you know that a little yeast leavens the whole batch of dough? Get rid of the old yeast, so that you may be a new unleavened batch—as you really are. For Christ, our Passover lamb, has been sacrificed. Therefore let us keep the Festival, not with the old bread leavened with malice and wickedness, but with the unleavened bread of sincerity and truth. 1 Corinthians 5:6-8

TIPS TO REMOVE INACTIVE YEAST SWIFTLY

- Address performance issues early.
- Communicate expectations always.
- Make connections.
- Be courageous to have difficult conversations and take difficult actions.
- Always listen to understand [grace] first and wrap the truth [salt] portion of the conversation with grace.

LESSON V: PLANTING SEEDS & FISHING

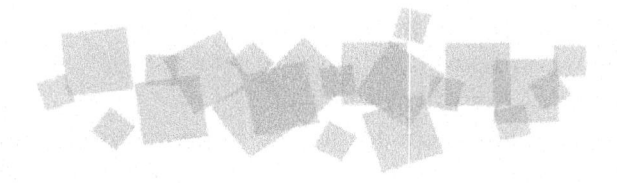

*Again he [Jesus] said, "What shall we say the kingdom
of God is like, or what parable shall we use to describe it?
It is like a mustard seed, which is the smallest seed you plant in the ground.
Yet when planted, it grows and becomes the largest of all garden plants,
with such big branches that the birds of the air can perch in its shade."*
Mark 4:30-32

I hate early flights. Why did I agree to a 6:00 a.m. flight to Dallas when it's an hour-plus to the airport? Leaving the house in the middle of the night is ridiculous. Well, that's the life of a travel warrior. Early morning flights and late-night dinners.

Are you serious? Not only do I hate early flights, but I hate small planes. Two seats on the left and one on the right. Please tell me I selected a one-seater? Nope. Two seats—but I've got a window seat. Well, at least I can get some sleep.

Groggy people walk like zombies onto the plane, put their bags in the overhead compartments, and take their seats one by one. Closing my eyes, I drift to sleep.

Something or "Someone" [God] prodded me to open my eyes. The guy next to me ordered a Bloody Mary with a beer chaser.

Odd. It's 6:00 a.m. on a Sunday morning and he's drinking already? Nice suit, but where have you been, buddy? Your eyes are really red.

Another one? He ordered another one?

Whoa! It's a short flight. I wonder if he's struggling with something.

I close my eyes and try to sleep.

Then, it happened. I peeked, and he caught my eye and started talking. *Really? It's 6:00 a.m. and you want to talk? Can't you see I want to sleep? I guess God put this man next to me for a reason.*

Sitting up in my seat, I engage in conversation.

"I'm on my way home from my niece's funeral," he said.

"Oh, I'm sorry. Are you okay?"

"Yeah, I guess. She was a drug addict and committed suicide. I'm still wearing the suit from the funeral. Didn't seem necessary to change."

He went on, "We handed these cards to everyone at the funeral. This is her picture. Beautiful girl. On the other side is the Serenity Prayer."

The Serenity Prayer by Reinhold Niebuhr[1]

God, grant me the serenity
to accept the things I cannot change,
the courage to change the things I can,
and the wisdom to know the difference.
Living one day at a time,
enjoying one moment at a time;
accepting hardship as a pathway to peace;
taking, as Jesus did,
this sinful world as it is,
not as I would have it;
trusting that You will make all things right
if I surrender to Your will;
so that I may be reasonably happy in this life
and supremely happy with You forever in the next.
Amen

"Take it. Give it to whoever needs it." He handed me the card.

"Thanks, I will." He continues to talk, and I listen until we make the final approach to the airport.

"Good luck," I said.

He smiles and waves as he walks to meet his wife.

Everyone has a story

This is a true story of a flight I'll never forget. Everyone has a story, and it's up to us to listen when they're ready to tell it.

Meeting this man, on that flight, at that time was a "God-moment." God chose me to help him process his niece's death while leaning on my faith. God gave me the words he needed to hear.

Are you wondering what happened to the card he gave me? Well, I gave it to another a few weeks later, as I promised.

5 STEPS TO PLANTING SEEDS & MAINTAINING PROPER TRAVELER'S ETIQUETTE

The next time you're sitting next to a stranger on a plane, a bus, or a train. Use these five steps.

1. Say "hello" and introduce yourself.
2. Notice how they respond. Do they tell you their name? Do they get out their book immediately? Do they have earbuds in? What about their body language?
3. If they don't start to read, watch a movie, or listen to music, they may want to talk. Start a conversation. If they start to read or listen to music, honor their decision.
4. Listen attentively. Why were they chosen to share your row? Do you need them, or do they need you?
5. Continue to plant seeds. Spread kindness and compassion wherever you go.

Planting seeds

We come into each other's lives to spread God's message by planting seeds. This man planted a seed with me, and I planted a seed with him.

Planting mustard seeds & teaching to fish

In Mark chapter 4 we learn about the parable of the growing mustard seed. This parable is similar to the saying "teach them to fish." Did you know that "teach them to fish" comes from a Chinese proverb? "Give a man a fish, feed him for a day; teach a man to fish, feed him for a lifetime."

Both Jesus's parable and the Chinese proverb are relevant in teaching your employees to make decisions, develop their skills, and advance within the organization.

Give a fish

When you teach employees to "fish," you empower them and build a culture of accountability. If you answer the employee's questions or *give* them a fish, they rely on you for answers in the future. They no longer are responsible for the outcome. If the decision wasn't the right one, the responsibility is yours. After all, you told them what to do.

When employees are conditioned or trained to depend upon their superiors to make decisions, business slows down, customer satisfaction declines, and employee engagement is minimal.

Give a fish scenario

Maria is a warranty claim representative at an online retailer.

Clicking away on her keyboard, she reviews the warranty claims in the queue.

Her phone rings. She reaches to her headset and says, "Hello. This is Maria. How can I help you?"

"Hi, Maria. This is Mike. I ordered a chain saw online but received a weed trimmer. I followed the proper procedures to return the chain saw, but it's been weeks and I haven't heard a word from anyone. The return number is 8546213, and it was shipped on August 23rd via UPS."

"Thanks, Mike. Let me pull up the order and see what's going on. Hmm, I see you ordered through a third-party online store. The return paperwork has been processed but is waiting supervisor approval. Unfortunately, my supervisor is on vacation and won't return for two more weeks. I'm sorry but we'll need to wait until they return."

"WHAT? Two more weeks? It's already been a month. This is ridiculous!" he says.

"I'm really sorry, Mike. But there isn't anything I can do without my supervisor's approval."

I hate it when I can't help a customer. I know he's super angry, and I don't blame him, but my hands are tied. I'll get in so much trouble if I approve the return without my supervisor's signature.

In this scenario, the supervisor is the ultimate decision-maker. The employees are to process warranty claims based on policy.

The supervisor "gives the fish" or decision because the employees' decisions are bound by the policy. They don't teach the employees "how to fish" or how to make decisions.

The supervisor built a culture of low trust between them and the employees. The employee strictly processes claims according to policy and nothing else.

"Teach employees to fish" culture

Teaching employees to fish means the leader teaches employees not only the job but, more importantly, how to make decisions and what decisions to make. The decisions align with the organization's culture.

"In the moment" decision-making

In the moment, it's easier to tell the employee the decision, and at that moment, it appears it's best for the customer, as well.

What if Maria's supervisor wasn't on vacation?

The customer is irate and wants an answer. She puts the customer on hold to talk to her supervisor, which makes the customer madder. No one likes to be put on hold.

Maria runs to her supervisor's office. She figures it's best to have this discussion in person so she gets an immediate response. This way, they can't let the phone go to voicemail if they don't want to answer.

Maria surprises Tony when she rushes into his office out of breath. "Hey, Tony. Sorry to bother you but I have an angry customer on the phone."

Tony looks up from his computer. "Hi, what's going on?"

Maria rushes through the situation as quickly as possible knowing the customer is still on hold and is ready to explode.

To make the situation and Maria go away, Tony quickly makes the decision, and Maria runs back to her desk to handle the call.

Tony returns to work, satisfied with how he handled the situation.

Missed lesson – shortsighted solution

Tony missed a perfect opportunity to teach the employee to fish. The way he handled the situation was shortsighted. In the moment, it made sense to quickly make a decision, but in doing so, Maria wasn't taught anything except to come to Tony each time she needs a decision made.

The customer was upset whether it took Maria two minutes or five minutes to get a final decision. The amount of time it took to get an answer should not have been the focus but, *in the moment*, both Tony and Maria wanted to get an answer to the customer as fast as possible. They focused on the wrong metric.

Lesson learned – long-term solution

The best course of action would have been for Tony to work through the decision-making process with Maria at that time. Helping her evaluate the situation and determine the best decision would "teach her to fish." And next time, she'd know the correct decision to make, therefore, helping the customer immediately.

The employee won't make a decision

What do you do if employees won't make decisions? Perhaps you've experienced when employees are reluctant to make decisions on their own or projects are delayed because the team struggles with making decisions. The leadership team states that the employees are autonomous, yet decisions aren't made at the employee level.

Why does this happen?

One reason is that supervisors, managers, and leadership *say* employees have autonomy to make decisions, but the *actions* of supervisors, managers, and leadership are not consistent with their words.

Tony and Maria's example shows how easy it is for a supervisor to make the decision for the employee. After all, an upset customer is on the phone, and we don't want them to hold too long.

If you were Tony, how would you handle this type of situation? What would be your inclination?

- Would you jump into decision-making mode?
- Would you calmly discuss the right course of action with the employee to train them for the next time?
- Would you make the decision but follow-up with the employee to discuss the rationale behind the decision and how the employee should handle the situation the next time?

> **HOW TO STOP THE URGE TO JUMP TO DECISION-MAKING MODE.**
>
> **TIP:** Write BREATHE, SEED, or FISH, on the whiteboard in your office. They are reminders to breathe, slow down, plant a seed, and teach them to fish. Also, write them on a sticky note and carry it with you.
>
> When an employee approaches you with a decision-making opportunity, look at those words to remind you it is a teaching moment. These words help to focus on the employee's growth and development and not on the decision.

Decision-making boundaries

To create a culture of accountability and trust, the supervisor teaches the employee the decision-making boundaries.

What are the parameters for the employee's decision-making authority?

Can Maria approve the product return without the supervisor's approval?

How many times can she do this?

Is she allowed to offer full refunds? Or should she offer a partial refund first, and if the customer is still unsatisfied, then they offer a full refund?

These are samples of decision-making boundaries that provide the employee's autonomy but still provide controls to avoid any financial surprises later.

Accountability reports

If you're still unsure about allowing employees to make decisions, one way to keep an eye on the potential financial ramifications is to create accountability reports.

Accountability reports provide details of the dollars the employee refunded to the customer. It shows the employee's name, date of transaction, amount of the refund or credit, and a reason code.

Send the report weekly to the team to track the dollars spent per employee.

Use the data to identify trends. Is one employee refunding more than the others? Is there a high refund rate for a specific product? Is there a quality issue? Does the employee need training?

Accountability reports are an important tool that allow employees autonomy but also keeps management aware of the dollars spent and why. The employee stays within their boundaries because they know the supervisor reviews their decisions.

Creating a safe environment

Creating a safe environment is critical in a "teach them to fish" culture. Employees must trust that the boss supports them in whatever decision they make. If their decision is wrong, the boss teaches the employee the right decision.

A safe environment removes the fear of being fired which allows the employee to think creatively and without hesitation.

Making decisions above the pay grade

Working in a safe environment includes the ability to make decisions "above the pay grade" or outside of their area of responsibility. If the situation needs immediate action, decisions must be made. This keeps business moving, encourages accountability, and increases employee engagement.

> **TIP: MAKING A DECISION ABOVE YOUR PAY GRADE**
>
> If you make a decision above your pay grade or outside of your area of responsibility, tell your boss and others involved immediately.
> Quick communication ensures no one is blindsided by the decision. It also provides an opportunity for the boss to teach if the decision wasn't ideal.

Planting mustard seeds

Planting mustard seeds starts with the smallest of seeds.

Talking to the man on my flight is an example of planting a seed. Another example is when standing in the checkout line at the grocery store, you make a comment to the person in front of you. The conversation continues and, suddenly, you tell them about a crazy thing that happened. The story or information shared needed to be heard. A mustard seed was planted. In the case of the grocery store, we'll never know how it impacted the other person, but it's our obligation to plant the seed.

Planting seeds with employees

Planting seeds with employees complements teaching them to fish. These two concepts work hand in hand in employee development. A seed is planted when the employee is encouraged to make decisions that impact the organization's future and their own. It's a development tool to evaluate employees' skills, create employee improvement plans, and intentionally develop the employee to reach career goals.

Be intentional with employee development.

Being intentional with employee development ensures the organization's future. To be intentional means to literally schedule time in your calendar to review your team's leadership skills and gaps. Create an employee growth plan that includes goals, gaps, actions, timelines, and responsibilities.

This is directly related to Greenleaf's definition of Servant Leadership in lesson III. "A servant-leader focuses primarily on the growth and well-being of people and the communities to which they belong. The servant-leader shares power, puts the needs of others first and helps people develop and perform as highly as possible."[2]

Colgate-Palmolive

William Colgate founded the Colgate company in 1806.[3] Colgate is over 200 years old and began making soaps and candles in New York City. In 2018, their worldwide net sales were $15.5 billion [USD]. Today, they have household brands of Colgate toothpaste, Soft Soap, Speed Stick, Murphy Oil Soap, and many others.[4]

Colgate's leadership philosophy

How did they continue to grow to a Fortune 500 company and sustain itself for over 200 years? Besides hard work and tough decisions, they had leaders who were intentional with the development of their employees.

- Prior to 1890 – Colgate gives financial support to Madison University in Hamilton, NY.
- In 1890, Madison University was renamed to Colgate University due to their longtime financial support of the institution.

From the beginning, Colgate considered education a critical component to employee's development.

Today, Colgate-Palmolive has established global leadership development programs including a corporate office internship program.

More than leadership development programs have contributed to Colgate's longevity and success, but without being intentional on planting seeds and teaching employees to fish, growing their organization would have been difficult.

Emerging leaders analysis

To begin the habit of intentionally identifying emerging leaders and understanding our own leadership skills and gaps, we need to conduct an evaluation.

Before we begin, download both the career assessment worksheet and the individual leadership skills assessment worksheet at www.graceandsaltbook.com/resources.

ACTIVITY: EMERGING LEADER ANALYSIS

LEADER'S PERSPECTIVE
[Download the *Grace & Salt* career assessment worksheet at www.graceandsaltbook.com under the resources tab.]

1. Write the name of each team member on the worksheet. It's important to actually write their names on a piece of paper. Writing causes us to think visually and removes distractions from the thought process.
2. Review the names. Is there an employee who demonstrates leadership skills? They may not lead a team but they demonstrate leadership skills in meetings or on projects. Providing creative ideas and influencing the team to follow their thoughts are attributes they possess. Are they your "go-to" person? What type of power do they have? Personal? Expert? Legitimate? *TIP: Pay attention to employees who have personal power. Employees with personal power have leadership tendencies.*
3. Identify the emerging leader(s).

ACTIVITY: EMERGING LEADER ANALYSIS (CONT.)

4. Schedule time with each emerging leader to discuss career goals. Discuss both *their* career goals and *your career goals for them*. Engagement increases, and the risk of losing a high-performing employee reduces.
    a. Establish expectations at the first meeting. Meeting goals, purpose, commitment to the plan, and timing are strong expectations for the career plan.
    b. Leadership Development Workshop Ideas: Communication styles, Building interpersonal relationships, Team building, and Executive presence.
5. Finalize the career assessment.
6. Identify gaps in their leadership skills and style.
7. Create a growth plan with the employee side by side. It's critical the relationship is built on trust with open and honest discussions. Share your thoughts, positive and negative, throughout the process.
8. Follow through and execute the plan. Remember this is a living document so adjustments are expected.
9. Celebrate along the way.

ACTIVITY: INDIVIDUAL LEADERSHIP SKILLS ASSESSMENT

EMPLOYEE'S PERSPECTIVE
[Download the *Grace & Salt* Individual Leadership Skills Assessment worksheet at www.graceandsaltbook.com under the resources tab.]

1. Write your name on a piece of paper and write the word *leader* next to it. It's important to write your name with *leader* next to it. Or write it on a sticky note and put it on your desk or in your planner to remind you that you are a *leader*. You have leadership skills that contribute to the organization daily.
2. Next, draw a line down the middle of the paper. Write "leadership skills" for the left-side column heading and "gaps" for the right-side column heading.
3. Complete each column based on your knowledge.
   - Take your time. This may take several days or weeks.
   - Find a trusted colleague or friend and ask them their opinion.

Pay attention in meetings on how you respond or don't respond to specific situations. Do you speak up at all meetings or only those where you're comfortable with the meeting participants? Do you speak up on conference calls but not in-person meetings? When faced with a challenge, how do you respond? Do you volunteer to lead? If you don't agree with a colleague, how do you respond?
These questions are intended to spark thoughts on your leadership skills.

4. Save this analysis for use later in this book.

Train the trainer

Today, we refer to a "teach them to fish" environment as "train the trainer." The leader plants the seed and cultivates [develops] the seed to grow. Through this process the leader continually teaches the employee to fish or trains the employee how to operate autonomously. This process repeats when the employee becomes a leader and repeats the process with their employees or co-workers, which fulfills the term "train the trainer."

The "train the trainer" concept builds a culture of accountability and responsibility, providing a long-term sustainable strategy, like Colgate-Palmolive. Jobs shape people, and a culture of accountability and responsibility shapes the employees generation after generation.

Wanting more decision-making responsibilities?

What if you want more decision-making responsibilities? Before we answer that question, we need to determine the trust level between you and your supervisor.

Low-trust environment

Does your boss repeatedly ask for the status of projects or control the outcome of a task? They want the activity completed exactly per their instructions. There isn't leeway to choose a different way to complete the task with the same outcome. Freedom is not in their vocabulary.

Basically, the supervisor doesn't trust the employee to complete the project or task without their involvement.

It's common for supervisors with low trust to micromanage. They manage into the details from a micro level and not from a macro level.

High-trust environment

In high-trust environments, there is freedom for the employee to choose how to complete a task or project. The supervisor provides the assignment's goals and objectives as well as the expectations.

Once the details are agreed upon, the employee(s) conducts the work, provides status updates, and communicates consistently to be sure they are on track to meet the deadline and expectations. A high-trust environment creates high employee engagement. The supervisor manages at a macro level.

HOW TO ASK FOR DECISION-MAKING RESPONSIBILITIES

Here are steps to prepare for the conversation in a high-trust relationship or environment:
1. Identify decisions that you are prepared to make.
2. Identify the positive impact a change in decision-making authority will have on your supervisor, the company, and the customer. How will it speed up the process? How will it impact customer satisfaction? How will it relieve your supervisor's workload?
3. Anticipate your supervisor's response and provide answers to the possible objections.
4. Determine the training required. Will you need additional training to ensure the decisions made will be aligned with the supervisor's and organization's expectations while building trust with you and your supervisor?

How to build trust in a low-trust environment

Consider these questions to build trust in a low-trust environment.

- If your supervisor micromanages, put yourself in their role. Do they need daily reports? Consistent communication? What concerns can you remove?
- What is it that makes them micromanage? What's their background? Were they burned by a previous employee? Does their boss micromanage? How can you relieve their stress?
- Would they allow you to make smaller decisions?
- What type of reports would help keep track of decisions made and potential impact to the organization?
- How can you make their life better?

Decision making & trust building

Teaching employees to make decisions and take risks takes time. It's most successful when built in a high-trust environment. Trust builds a culture of accountable and highly engaged employees.

According to Stephen M.R. Covey, it's proven that by creating an environment of trust and accountability, business speed is increased and customer satisfaction is improved.[5]

He says, when "trust goes down, speed will also go down and costs will go up."[6] The opposite is also true. "When trust goes up, speed goes up and costs go down."

When decisions are made faster, the employee becomes more engaged because there is a sense of ownership.

Imagine how Maria would have felt if she resolved the customer's issue right away. Her engagement would have increased substantially knowing that *she* resolved the customer's issue.

THE CONVERSATION GUIDE.
5 STEPS TO AN EFFECTIVE MEETING WITH THE BOSS

1. Find two open times on the supervisor's schedule.
   a. Choose the best time of day when the supervisor is the most relaxed and available both mentally and physically. Morning? Late afternoon?
   b. Choose the best day of the week.
   c. Allow 45 – 60 minutes. This allows for interruptions and if the supervisor is late or needs to leave early.
2. Call the supervisor to ask for a few minutes, suggest two dates and times, and tell them the topic.
   a. It's best to call rather than e-mail. E-mail may get lost or misinterpreted.
   b. Two meeting options provide choices and gives them control of the date.
3. Once the meeting time is scheduled, send a meeting invitation.
4. Determine the best choice based on the supervisor's style: a formal presentation or a casual conversation.
5. Focus the conversation on how you can help and relieve their stress and workload. It isn't about gaining more responsibility and control.

Sense of pride & accomplishment

There is one more point I want to make. When a supervisor makes decisions for the employee, not only do they train the employee to seek others for decisions, but they also rob the employee the satisfaction of resolving the problem themself. This is critical.

> **THE SUPERVISOR ROBS THE EMPLOYEE OF THE SATISFACTION OF RESOLVING THE PROBLEM.**

When employees make decisions and solve problems, they feel a sense of accomplishment. They feel good about themselves, and this builds confidence.

Have you ever built something by hand? Perhaps you paid for your first car without help from your parents. How did it feel when you pulled the car into the driveway? How did it feel when you finished crocheting the blanket for a friend or making a special bird feeder for your mom?

This is the same pride your employees feel when they accomplish a task, project, or make a decision. When we make the decision for them or take the decision out of their hands, we rob them of a sense of pride and an opportunity to grow.

Employee development plan

Before completing the employee development plan, be aware that not every employee aspires to be a supervisor.

Although we've spent time discussing cultures of accountability and autonomy, some employees aren't comfortable making decisions. And others need to build confidence or feel safe in the decision-making process. Keep this in mind when completing the Employee Development Plan.

EMPLOYEE DEVELOPMENT PLAN MATRIX

Grace & Salt leadership competencies: Communication, Customer focus, Courage or risk-taking, Listening skills, Community, and Connections or teamwork.

Following is a sample development matrix.

The downloadable version is available at www.graceandsaltbook.com/resources.

The matrix:

- Identifies the employee's (or your) gaps in each competency and decision-making ability.
- Identifies potential successor(s).
- Identifies the employee's (or your) potential advancement.

After completion, identify the areas of improvement and establish a development plan in each gap area.
Review the development plan with each employee to gain acceptance and alignment. Their input creates a stronger plan with a higher success rate.

REFER TO MY WEBSITE,
WWW.GRACEANDSALTBOOK.COM,
FOR A SAMPLE EMPLOYEE DEVELOPMENT PLAN
(FOUND UNDER THE "RESOURCES" TAB)

Here's the background on the employees in the sample Employee Development Plan:

- **Susan** is an employee who occasionally makes decisions on her own. The supervisor believes she's uncomfortable making decisions and rates her a 3 (somewhat evident).
- **John** is an employee who makes decisions frequently and

appears to be comfortable with decision making. He is rated a 5 (expertly applies decision making).

Development matrix evaluation of Susan

Further evaluation is required to understand if Susan isn't comfortable making decisions or if she's been conditioned to not make decisions on her own.

- Is it her personality?
- Does she feel safe in making decisions? Will her supervisor support her if she's wrong?
- Has she made wrong decisions in the past and was reprimanded?
- Is the department's culture one where employees don't make decisions without the supervisor's approval?

Employees who seek validation

Some employees want validation that their decision is right, or they want a supervisor to agree before they make the decision. Waiting for the supervisor's response via e-mail, voice mail, or in-person slows business down.

Three reasons why employees don't make decisions

The first reason is that the employee isn't comfortable making decisions. They know the correct course of action but aren't risk-takers and want to be sure the supervisor knows of the situation and supports their action plan.

The second reason is the organization's culture isn't a safe place. The employee had a bad experience where they were reprimanded. Because of that experience they learned and decided to seek the supervisor's approval for all decisions.

The third reason is they weren't taught how to make a decision.

Most of us learn through observing. Observing others teaches the authority we have and the course of action to take.

In many circumstances, supervisors don't train employees on how to make decisions or the decision-making boundaries.

Active teaching

Observation and experience are examples of passive learning. For the majority of employees to be comfortable making decisions, active teaching is required.

Active teaching is when a supervisor or leader actively teaches another employee. This is an intentional action to improve the employee's skills and understandings.

In the development plan matrix, Susan is rated a three in decision-making ability. Active teaching would ask questions to determine the root cause behind her hesitancy to make decisions.

Once the root cause is determined, it's easier to create a development plan.

- Why is she rated a three?
- Why does she make decisions sometimes but not all the time?
- Observe her behavior. When does she make decisions and when doesn't she? Is there a pattern?
- During a decision-making discussion, ask her what she thinks the right decision is for that specific situation. Have her make the decision.
- When appropriate, discuss her reluctance to make decisions. Dig into the reason(s) why she hesitates. This is the first step in understanding how to improve this area for Susan.
- Open communication filled with grace and salt provides a natural atmosphere that removes awkwardness or concern from Susan.

If she absolutely is not comfortable with decision making at any level and the job requires it, consider another role for Susan.

Development matrix exercise

It's time for you to complete the development matrix for you and your team.

The matrix provides a complete evaluation of the team members and highlights the strengths and gaps in their leadership growth.

Use the sample matrix on the previous pages to guide you through the process.

If you do not lead a team, complete the matrix for yourself.

DEVELOPMENT MATRIX INSTRUCTIONS

Rating scale: 1 (not evident) to 5 (expertly applied).

1. Complete the matrix for each employee.
2. Complete the action step section to identify areas of improvement, timelines, and responsibility.
3. Discuss the plan with each employee to get feedback and alignment.
4. Schedule progress meetings in your calendars immediately.
5. Prioritize the development plan to the top of the list. The plan and meetings are sacred.

Note: Reference the competency descriptions in the matrix to understand each section.

DON'T FORGET TO VISIT MY WEBSITE, WWW.GRACEANDSALTBOOK.COM, TO DOWNLOAD A SAMPLE EMPLOYEE DEVELOPMENT PLAN UNDER THE "RESOURCES" TAB.

Lesson V: Be intentional in the creation of development paths for employees. Incorporate active teaching into your leadership style.

Specifically, teach the decision-making process and boundaries while creating a safe environment for risk-taking.

Again he [Jesus] said, "What shall we say the kingdom of God is like, or what parable shall we use to describe it? It is like a mustard seed, which is the smallest seed you plant in the ground. Yet when planted, it grows and becomes the largest of all garden plants, with such big branches that the birds of the air can perch in its shade." Mark 4:30-32

LESSON VI: PRAY UNTIL SOMETHING HAPPENS (PUSH)

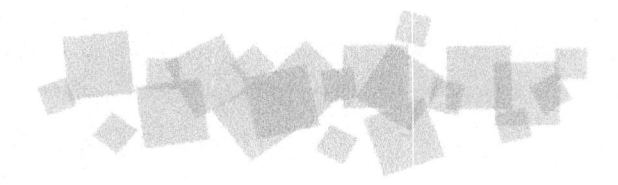

Pray continually.
1 Thessalonians 5:17

The final piece in this leadership analysis is prayer. The world is a busy place which is not much different than in Jesus's day.

In 1 Thessalonians, Paul encourages the Thessalonian church to continue their Christian work. Thessalonica was a busy seaport city at the head of the Thermaic Gulf. It was considered an important communication and trade center.[1]

In this busy city, the new Christians were surrounded by evil and pagan activities. The Thessalonica residents were members of religious cults and worshiped Roman and Egyptian gods.[2] The new church members needed encouragement and reminders that their responsibilities were to spread Christianity and welcome new members to the church.

Wouldn't that be awesome? To receive encouragement to move forward with our responsibilities. What if we received encouragement and reminders of our ultimate responsibility to spread Christianity?

It's easy to be distracted by the whirlwind of life and prioritize activities and daily tasks above talking to God.

Protection

Paul reminds us in 1 Thessalonians 5:8-11:

"But since we belong to the day, let us be self-controlled, putting on faith and love as a breastplate, and the hope of salvation as a helmet. For God did not appoint us to suffer wrath but to receive salvation through our Lord Jesus Christ. He died for us so that, whether we are awake or asleep, we may live together with him. Therefore, encourage one another and build each other up, just as in fact you are doing."

You may be familiar with the armor of God from Ephesians 6:10-18 and its direction to protect yourself against the enemy. This is another reference to the armor of God with faith and love as the breastplate and helmet of salvation. Paul's reference in 1 Thessalonians is a little different than the armor referenced in Ephesians, but it is the same thought. We must be protected and gather together to beat the evil one.

Encouragement

In addition to the armor protecting us, we also need to *"encourage one another and build each other up."* In the workplace and personal relationships, friends or colleagues don't often build each other up. Many times, covert workplace battles take place where colleagues focus on moving up the corporate ladder and disregard those they step on during the assent. This was not God's intent for His people. Our instructions are to build one another up and mentor each other so that we can fight another day together.

Prayer

We've talked about filling all conversations with grace & salt, building a sense of belonging, and incorporating servant leadership attributes into our leadership styles while finding ways to give to our communities. Planting seeds, teaching employees to fish, and establishing employee development plans encourage one another and build each other up. Another way is through prayer, focusing on raising up your friends, colleagues, and loved ones to God in praise and love.

Paul's final instructions

As we move through 1 Thessalonians, Paul writes the final instructions to the Thessalonian church:

> *"Now we ask you, brothers and sisters, to acknowledge those who work hard among you, who care for you in the Lord and who admonish you. Hold them in the highest regard in love because of their work. Live in peace with each other.*
>
> *And we urge you, brothers and sisters, warn those who are idle and disruptive, encourage the disheartened, help the weak, be patient with everyone. Make sure that nobody pays back wrong for wrong, but always strive to do what is good for each other and for everyone else.*
>
> *Rejoice always, pray continually, give thanks in all circumstances; for this is God's will for you in Christ Jesus."*[3] 1 Thessalonians 5:12-18

This passage gives specific instructions on how to treat others.

- Encourage everyone not just those we like or connect with.

Notice Paul says to acknowledge those who admonish you. It's important to not only recognize those who agree but also those who disagree with you. Those people in your life who give you counsel or scold you for a specific action or direction.

- Encourage and acknowledge those who work hard and care for you.
- Talk to those who are idle or not doing anything. This includes those employees who are going "through the motions" and are not fully engaged.

- Have difficult conversations with those employees who are poor performers or not engaged in their work.
- Be patient with each other and don't allow ourselves or others to pay back a wrong for a wrong.
- Do what is right for each other.
- Always be joyful, always be praying, and always be thankful.

PUSH – A REMINDER TO PRAY CONTINUOUSLY

Pray Continually. Pray Until Something Happens or PUSH! Many years ago, I heard a sermon on the acronym PUSH. The message was to Pray Until Something Happens (PUSH), pray without ceasing, or pray continually. Paul tells us to pray continually or pray until something happens and then pray some more. As a reminder, the next time you are at the store and see PUSH on the door, think about this acronym.

Prayer life

As you begin or enhance your prayer life, write down your prayer requests. It's probable that God answered your prayers but life's busyness prevented you from seeing them.

I encourage you to pray in your workplace, in your office, in conference rooms, or wherever you're comfortable.

Starting the day asking God to provide courage, wisdom, and words to face challenges and interactions during the day changes your mindset and outlook. Knowing He is at your side facing difficulties and providing directions to complex decisions gives a reassurance that's unexplainable.

Isaiah 42:6 says, *"I, the Lord, have called you in righteousness. I will take hold of your hand."* How amazing! *He* will hold my hand (and yours) throughout this day. No matter what. How incredible and comforting! I am not alone. We are not alone.

> REFLECTION TIME:
> SPEND SOME QUIET TIME REFLECTING AND PRAYING.

SEVEN STEPS TO INCORPORATE PRAYER INTO YOUR WORKDAY

1. Block off fifteen minutes on your calendar each morning for prayer and journaling. Mark it as Do Not Disturb.
2. Find a quiet space at home (if working remotely) or at your workplace.
3. Take out your Grace & Salt Journal and download the journal prompts at www.graceandsaltbook.com
4. Pray. Ask God to provide insight as you read. Ask the Holy Spirit to join you and open your mind, ears, eyes, and heart to His instructions and messages.
5. If you have a specific book of the Bible you'd like to read, start there. If not, just open the Bible and start reading. Many of us think linearly so we start at the beginning. But that's not always the best place to start. Let God lead you. He knows the message you need to hear. Trust Him.
6. Journal. Write down thoughts, messages, and instructions you hear. Read aloud, if necessary, to remove distracting thoughts.
7. Close the session by praying for your workplace, colleagues, decisions, courage, wisdom, discussions, co-workers, and leaders. Pray for company leaders and that God provides courage for the decisions they face and that they keep Him at the focus of the decisions.

Lesson VI: Remember Paul's three commands:

Always be joyful
always be praying,
and always be thankful.

Pray Until Something Happens (PUSH).

"Pray continually." 1 Thessalonians 5:17

SECTION I: GRACE & SALT LEADERSHIP SUMMARY

I hope you've enjoyed the first section of this book. My promise is that if you invest the time and energy to complete the activities, assessments, and evaluations, you'll have a complete plan to build a culture of serving, accountability, responsibility, and an environment full of passionate employees.

Following is a guide to remind you of the lessons we reviewed. Feel free to print, laminate, and carry it with you.

Download it at www.graceandsaltbook.com under the resources tab.

- **I: G & S –** *Grace & Salt*. Blend grace and salt based on the circumstances and relationship with the other person(s) and wrap the conversation in grace regardless of the amount of salt needed. Have all conversations filled with grace and seasoned with salt (truth). (Colossians 4:6)
- **II:** *Connections & Sense of Belonging*. Build an environment filled with a sense of belonging and trust through Paul's method of connecting with one another. (1 Corinthians 9:22)
- **III:** *Serving & Giving*. Incorporate servant leadership into your leadership style by putting employees first. Be intentional with incorporating serving and giving into your personal and

professional lives. Become active in local charities. Choose to lead with a servant-heart and be a generous giver of your time, talents, and resources. (Mark 10:45)

- *IV: Remove Inactive Yeast Swiftly.* Remove inactive yeast (underperforming employees) swiftly to positively impact the team and organization. Use the power matrix to understand the types of power employees' possess and if they use it in the best interest of the company. Inactive yeast slows business down, and delaying the removal may rob the employee of finding their true purpose. (1 Corinthians 5:6-8)
- *V: Planting Seeds & Fishing.* Be intentional in the development path of the employees. Teach them how to make decisions & the boundaries for those decisions while creating a safe environment for risk-taking. It's important for the company's growth and longevity to ensure a strong succession program for all roles in the organization. Reference the Parable of the Mustard Seed (Mark 4:26-34) and the Chinese proverb: Give a man a fish, feed him for a day; teach a man to fish, feed him for a lifetime.
- *VI: Pray Continually.* Incorporate prayer into your workday. Remember Paul's three commands: Always be joyful, always be praying, and always be thankful. Pray Until Something Happens (PUSH). (1 Thessalonians 5:16-18)

Congratulations! You deserve a break. When you're ready, come back and let's focus on you, the leader, and how to survive the chaos of leadership.

SECTION II – THE LEADER — HOW TO MAINTAIN AND SURVIVE THE CHAOS

Welcome back! Like with most leadership development books, it takes time and energy to understand and implement the concepts.

This next section focuses on the leader and how to survive the chaos of leadership. It includes six lessons that apply to both new leaders and experienced leaders.

Let's start by understanding a typical day of a leader. Many leaders relate to the statement that *sleep is restless and brief*. They may physically spend six to eight hours in bed, but they don't actually sleep.

If they do, it's not the good REM sleep that everyone talks about. Typically, they toss and turn and can't turn off their brain. So much to do and so little time.

I love getting to the office early. Going through my e-mail inbox before the day "really" starts is satisfying. Rushing out the door, I grab my keys and phone. *Wait! Where's my phone? There it is. On the nightstand.*

Oh boy, a text message from the boss. An emergency meeting? It's at the same time as our marketing meeting. This is the umpteenth time I've had to reschedule a meeting and put my plans on hold because "someone" else's emergency becomes my emergency.

Fine. Whatever. I better not check my blood pressure. I'm sure it's through the roof.

Does this sound familiar? My guess is that this type of morning is similar to what you've experienced.

The schedule is planned, and a boss derails it. You'll need to figure out how to get your work done another time and another day. Lunch and breaks are rare, and quality time with your family is nonexistent. You're on call 24/7/365, being tossed around like a tennis ball.

If this describes a typical day, you'll enjoy this next section. These six lessons focus on your self-care and teach you how to stay focused and energized among the madness.

If you don't care for yourself, you won't be able to care for others. Lesson III, Serving and Giving, introduced servant leadership. But the danger of servant leadership and serving others is that you may forget to serve yourself.

It's okay to schedule time to focus on *your* self-care.

I'm not sure where you're at in your life or career right now. You might be feeling on top of the world and are reading this book to enhance your leadership style and skills. Or you may be exhausted and ready to give up.

Regardless of where you're at, this next section teaches how to care for yourself and fight another day.

There are six main areas we'll discuss in this section:

- **VII. Temptation** — Use Power for Good — Relationships, Focus, & Pride
- **VIII. Courage** — Be Like Esther: Stand Up, Step Out, Speak Up
- **IX. Refresh Yourself** — Take a Spiritual Personal Activity (SPA) Day
- **X. Self-awareness and Growth** — The New You
- **XI. Mentor** — Have One, Be One
- **XII. Prayer** — The Power of Prayer in Leadership

Let's get started.

LESSON VII: TEMPTATION — USE YOUR POWER FOR GOOD

Love the Lord your God with all your heart and with all your soul and with all your strength. These commandments that I give you today are to be upon your hearts. Impress them on your children. Talk about them when you sit at home and when you walk along the road, when you lie down and when you get up. Tie them as symbols on your hands and bind them on your foreheads. Write them on the doorframes of your houses and on your gates.
Deuteronomy 6:5-9

Temptation. We'll focus on three areas of temptation: relationships, losing focus, and pride. Why am I starting with temptation?

Well, surviving the chaos of leadership requires the awareness of temptations. Understanding what they are, how they impact your life, and how to deal with them moves you forward.

If you've been impacted by temptation in relationships, you know it can upset lives and at times ruin relationships. If we lose focus and get distracted through temptation, it slows business and derails career plans while temptation to pride or ego distracts from fulfilling our purpose.

Discussing these topics brings awareness so that we recognize the temptation and remove it before it hurts or derails our purpose.

Deuteronomy 6:5 instructs us to *"love the Lord your God with all your heart and with all your soul and with all your strength.* Focusing on God in every situation, no matter how strong the temptation is, gives us the power to remove it.

Temptation — Relationships

Work-Life balance or blend

Work-life balance is an overused and inaccurate phrase. Is it really balanced?

The definition of balance is "stability produced by even distribution of weight on either side of the vertical axis."[1] In other words, 50% of the weight on each side of the scale. Is this how you would describe your life? 50% of your work life on one side of the scale, and 50% of your home life on the other side?

Typically, our work life and home life aren't completely balanced. One life outweighs the other and becomes imbalanced.

Work-home blending is more accurate. Sometimes the focus is at home if you're a new parent or the kids are sick.

Other times, the focus is on work where deadlines or business trips take you away from home.

Recognizing and acknowledging that at times home life may not get as much attention as you'd like may leave you feeling guilty. To deal with the guilt, one strategy is to practice being totally present when at home.

Relationships & being totally present

Being totally present. How do you do that?

Years ago, I heard a speaker introduce the concept of being totally present at all times. The idea is to be totally present wherever you are. To focus 100% on the person(s) you're with regardless if you're at work or at home.

People know when you're distracted and thinking of other things, especially if you're checking your phone each time it pings.

How to remove distractions

Cell phones, tablets, computers, e-mails, social media, and text messages are examples of distractions that prevent us from being totally present.

In the 1890s, Ivan Pavlov, a Russian scientist, proved that dogs can be conditioned to salivate when they heard a noise. He did this through a series of events where each time he sounded a metronome, he fed the dogs.

Eventually, the dogs salivated when they heard the metronome even when no food was given or seen. This is Pavlovian conditioning.

Let's adapt this concept to how we respond to our devices. Have you been Pavlovian conditioned?

To most people, their cell phone or computer's notification sound has conditioned them to check their device. They've become Pavlovian conditioned.

HAVE YOU BEEN (PAVLOVIAN) CONDITIONED?

- When your device pings, do you look at it (even a glance)?
- Do you check your device once every ten minutes? Thirty minutes?
- Do you check your device during conversations?
- If you've answered yes to any of the above, you are Pavlovian conditioned.

HOW TO TRAIN YOURSELF TO BE TOTALLY PRESENT

DEVICE ETIQUETTE

- Put your device in your car, purse, or out of sight when with family members.
- Put your device on silent when with family, in a meeting, or in a conversation.
- Flip your device upside down or close it to remove the temptation of distraction.
- When unavailable, enable the "out of office" e-mail feature. Use this feature even for meetings, especially if you're expecting an important message.
- Enable the "do not disturb" function on your cell phone. To allow important callers (spouse, children, boss) to bypass the system, categorize them as favorites in contacts.
- Schedule specific times to check e-mail. And only check e-mail at the scheduled times. This technique increases productivity.

Conversation Etiquette (Family or Colleague)

- Deliberately focus on the conversation. If the mind wanders, repeat the other person's words silently to remove distracting thoughts.
- Practice active listening. Repeat what they've said back to them to ensure you've heard correctly.

How to address a friend or colleague if they *aren't* listening

- Remember a conversation where the other person wasn't listening. The other person was nodding their head, but their thoughts were clearly elsewhere. How did you feel? How did you respond?
- Simply say, "You seem distracted. What's on your mind?" This approach tells the other person to pay attention without creating conflict and gives them an opportunity to address their thoughts, if necessary. We're all busy, and offering grace shows that you care about whatever is on their mind.

Now we know we are conditioned.
Let's spend time eliminating the temptation.

Complete the Totally Present Brainstorming Activity to identify ideas to become an expert at being totally present.

TOTALLY PRESENT BRAINSTORMING ACTIVITY

1. Turn off your device or put it on silent. Turn it over to remove distractions.
2. Take a piece of paper and think about ways to become totally present with friends and family.
3. Set a clock for five minutes.
4. Write down every idea that comes to your mind, even if it's crazy, silly, or stupid.
5. Answer these questions: How can I be engaged and truly listen? What can I do to keep my mind from wandering?
6. When finished, circle the ideas that make sense and align with your personality style. Be intentional on how to incorporate one or two into conversations with family and friends.
7. Record and track your progress on a journal page. Recording and celebrating is critical to establish the habit. You can use the journal page available at www.graceandsaltbook.com/resources.

Being totally present is a skill that takes time to perfect and enhances relationships both at home and at work.

Relationships & gossip

"What a day! I need a break."

I'm going upstairs to the break room. Taking one step at a time and breathing with each step, I try to calm down. I get a Diet Coke out of the pop machine and squeeze into a chair trying to make room at the table and let off some steam.

"This morning has been hectic! The phone won't stop ringing. You'd think that Jane would answer a few calls rather than talking to John. It's the end of the month, and we have tons of paperwork to get done. Jane makes me..."

Jane walks into the break room.

I stop talking as I feel the blood flush from my neck to the top of my head.

Did she hear me? She most definitely did. What do I do? How embarrassing! Why do I do that? It never fails. Whenever I start talking about someone, they walk into the room. Haven't I learned my lesson?

A murmur fills the room, and the ladies start to talk about nothing to fill the awkward silence. I slowly get up with my head down and walk back to my office feeling awful for what I said.

Does this scenario resonate with you? Have you been caught gossiping?

Gossip is dangerous and doesn't bring value to the discussion or your reputation. Frustration is expected when working with others, but your response to the frustration is what's important. Gossip is not the appropriate response.

My relationship with Jane was hurt that day. I didn't want that to happen. She was my friend and a great co-worker, but giving in to my frustration and publicly talking about her showed my immaturity and hurt my reputation. I apologized to her right away and hoped it restored our friendship.

The lesson I learned and am sharing with you is to think twice the next time the temptation to gossip appears.

HOW TO REMOVE THE TEMPTATION TO GOSSIP

Take a breath before you speak and ask yourself these questions:

- What will happen to the relationship if I gossip?
- What is the value in repeating the story to another person?
- Will anyone benefit from the story?
- What's the point of repeating it?
- What will others think of me and how will it impact my reputation?

Then, don't open your mouth, go back to work, or share information of value. Celebrate internally that you beat the temptation to gossip!

Relationships & forgiveness

So what happens if you give into temptation and hurt a relationship? What do you do? First, determine how to recover the relationship and rebuild trust.

In the above example with Jane, the first step was to apologize. The next step was to ask for forgiveness. When giving into temptation, oftentimes it's followed by asking for forgiveness or offering forgiveness if on the receiving end of the offense.

Forgiveness provides a sense of freedom and allows you to "release resentment."[2] "The act of forgiveness is first and foremost for ourselves. It lets us move on from the past instead of letting bitterness and anger to perturb our emotional well-being."[3]

Notice how this quote focuses on the future and isn't about holding on to the past. Asking for forgiveness from my co-worker helped us move on.

Or did it? She accepted my apology and forgave me, but I never forgave myself. Thirty years have passed, and I'm still talking about it.

Forgiving ourselves

To some of us, forgiving others comes more naturally than forgiving ourselves. What does Jesus say about forgiveness? The Bible tells us that God forgives us. He sent Jesus to die for our sins, and if we ask for forgiveness, He will forgive us. The Bible teaches that we should forgive others in the same way that God forgives us.

Ephesians 4:31-32 states *"Get rid of all bitterness, rage and anger, brawling and slander, along with every form of malice. Be kind and compassionate to one another, forgiving each other, just as in Christ God forgave you."*

Mark 11:25 says [Jesus says] *"And when you stand praying, if you hold anything against anyone, forgive him, so that your Father in heaven may forgive you your sins."*

There are countless examples of where God or Jesus instructs us to forgive others. However, the Bible doesn't address forgiving yourself.

The guilt is immeasurable when you do or say something stupid.

Well, it's time to forgive ourselves right now and offer ourselves grace. I won't forget it, but I will forgive it.

God forgives us so we should forgive ourselves. Jeremiah 31:34 states that *"For I will forgive their wickedness and I will remember their sins no more."* God forgives our sins and removes them from His memory.

So if God forgives our sins, then why can't we forgive ourselves?

It's not about *forgetting* the sin. It's about *forgiving* it. Remembering it helps to not repeat it. Learn from the mistake and remember. This is contrary to the phrase "forgive and forget." After all, when you ask God for forgiveness, He wipes you clean and forgets the sin. Thank God He forgets my sins and wipes me clean.

However, forgetting past sins allows for the past to be repeated. We don't learn from them. Every time I have the temptation to gossip, I think about Jane. It causes me to stop and ask the questions above.

Forgive yourself by letting go of it. Stop allowing a past decision to control you. Change your behavior, ask God and others for forgiveness, and forgive yourself.

"Philippians 4:9 states that we are to put into practice those things that we have learned from God and from His Word. To continue to rehearse in our thoughts the events of our transgression, opposes Philippians 4:8 which tells us to dwell on whatever is true, noble, right, pure, lovely, and admirable"[4]

What are you holding on to no matter how big or small?

Begin right now. Forgive yourself and change your behavior.

> Focus your attention and power on good deeds, relationships, building trust, and spreading God's Word through your actions.
> Use your power for good and not evil.

Temptation — Losing focus and distractions

So I sent messengers to them with this reply, "I am carrying on a great project and cannot go down. Why should the work stop while I leave it and go down to you?"
Nehemiah 6:3

Years ago, my boss had a philosophy that you should work on everything a little bit each day. That way all priorities move inch by inch toward completion. At the time, it made sense. It was a typical environment of "keep all of the plates spinning."

Picture a juggler who is spinning three, four, five, or six plates on wooden sticks. Each plate represents an activity, project, program, or task. The juggler holds several in his hands and then starts to use his feet. Been there? Know how the juggler feels?

This philosophy moves projects along but at a slow pace. The sense of accomplishment never comes because nothing gets completed. Keeping "all of the plates spinning" is exhausting. When a "plate" falls, it's demotivating and disappointing.

Writing this book

This book has been incubating in my mind and heart since 2014. Sitting down on weekends was challenging when thoughts about work, chores, or watching a tennis match distracted me. Distractions were there every time I sat down to write. Giving in to the distractions is one reason it took years to complete.

Traveling to Spain for a few days of focus helped, but distractions were still all around. When I realized that the outline was rooted in God's plan for me, you'd think it would have driven me to complete it in record time. But it wasn't until late 2016 that I found a cadence to write.

Making excuses was a great delay tactic. "To write, you need to travel to a secluded place to remove distractions," I'd think. If I were secluded, there wouldn't be any distractions. Right? I researched the cost of remote cabins in the Rocky Mountains or Tennessee. I thought about visiting my sister in Florida. The actual thought of traveling to a "secluded place" became the distraction.

This book was delayed because I made excuses. God's plan was delayed because I made excuses.

Does that happen to you? You establish a goal and talk about it, but no progress is made. Excuses become the reason why you're not moving forward, but the excuses are the reason no progress is made.

Finally, I decided to write on Sundays. The Sunday writing ritual continued for years with small doses of progress. I felt good because although progress was slow, there was still progress. The distractions I was choosing instead of writing were good things. It didn't seem wrong or bad because my choices were good things, but they weren't aligned with God's plan.

When good choices delay God's choices

Publishing this book was God's plan for the second half of my life.

Rather than concentrating on completing the book, I decided to finish a master's degree early.

Finishing the master's degree appeared to be a good decision, but it distracted me from God's plan. Taking two courses per semester consumed my time. Writing this book became a low priority. My intention was good. On the surface it made sense, but it delayed the completion of this book. Taking one course at a time would have allowed time to focus on the book and school. After all, the graduation date was the same whether I finished in March or May.

This "good" decision [distraction] delayed the publishing of this book at least three months. In other words, this [reasonable, good] decision delayed God's purpose [writing this book] a minimum of three months.

We choose our focus and distractions. Distractions are a choice.

Nehemiah's lesson on focus and prioritization

Reflect on your life currently.

Are all of the plates spinning? Is there something you've delayed because other activities are getting your attention? Do you feel that "pull" to start something, to stop something, or to finish something? How are you prioritizing your activities?

Nehemiah was a Jewish leader and the cupbearer for King Artaxerxes, the king of Persia. A king's cupbearer was responsible to serve the wine at the king's table. To ensure that the king was not poisoned, the cupbearer drank the wine first.[5]

Can you imagine? On one hand you have access to the king, but on the other hand, you may be poisoned and die. Nehemiah was a trusted cupbearer to King Artaxerxes.

One day, he received news that the walls of Jerusalem were destroyed, and the gates burned. Being Jewish and knowing that Jerusalem was chosen by King David to be the Holy Temple, he was concerned that Jerusalem would be defenseless and appear as a ruined city without a proper wall or gates.

Jerusalem was where Nehemiah's father and family were buried. It was important that Jerusalem be rebuilt to honor his family and God.

"Broken Windows" concept

Nehemiah practiced the concept of "broken windows." Replacing broken windows, cleaning up garbage, and renewing abandoned buildings and neighborhoods instills pride into the area. Businesses open, crime decreases, and residents return.

If the neighborhood remains in ruins, the opposite happens. Crime increases, businesses close, and residents move away.

This is the "broken windows" concept.

On a smaller scale, the idea of "broken windows" is to repair whatever is broken, pick up trash, and respect buildings whether it's your office building or your home. First impressions are critical, and customers or visitors get a negative impression if the building inside or outside isn't cared for.

This was the reason Nehemiah wanted to repair Jerusalem's wall.

Nehemiah asks the king to rebuild the wall

Nehemiah wanted to personally lead the reconstruction of the wall and gates but needed King Artaxerxes's permission. So, he prayed to God that he would be granted permission and "favor" of the king.

To speak to the king, he needed the "king's favor." This means he needed the king's attention without upsetting him. If you approached the king without permission, death was possible. Nehemiah knew the risk and took it. After his prayer, he handed the king a cup of wine, and the king noticed that Nehemiah seemed sad, which was unlike him.

"What's wrong, Nehemiah?" the king asked.

It's interesting how Nehemiah didn't have to approach the king. The king approached Nehemiah and gave him an opening to explain the situation. Nehemiah courageously told the king his plan to lead the rebuilding efforts and asked if the king would communicate with the area kings to ensure safe passage to Jerusalem. King Artaxerxes agreed to everything Nehemiah requested.

Nehemiah stays focused

Nehemiah's lesson on focus begins in Nehemiah 4:1.

Once the neighboring rulers discovered Nehemiah's plan, they were concerned. Having Jerusalem in shambles and defenseless was their preference. To stop Nehemiah, they plotted to kill everyone working on the reconstruction efforts.

Nehemiah continually prayed to God for safety. In Nehemiah 4:14, he reminds the workers, nobles, and officials, *"...Don't be afraid of them [enemies]. Remember the Lord, who is great and awesome, and fight for your brothers, your sons and your daughters, your wives and your homes."*

Nehemiah chooses focus and not distraction

He focused on the Lord's plan and prayed while he prepared for the potential attack. But his enemies continually tried to distract him.

However, in Nehemiah 6, it says, *"When word came to Sanballat, Tobiah, Geshem the Arab and the rest of our enemies that I had rebuilt the wall and not a gap was left in it—though up to that time I had not set the doors in the gates— Sanballat and Geshem sent me this message: 'Come, let us meet together in one of the villages on the plain of Ono.'"* (v. 1-2).

Nehemiah knew they planned to kill him. So, he replied, *"I am carrying on a great project and cannot go down. Why should the work stop while I leave it and go down to you?"* (v. 3). Four more times, they tried to convince him to come down. And Nehemiah gave the same answer. *"I am carrying on a great project and cannot go down."*

It was time for a different tactic. Sanballat and Geshem sent a different message claiming that Nehemiah planned to become the king of Judah and that was the reason he was rebuilding the wall. This wasn't the truth, but they were trying to entice him to come down to kill him.

What a creative tactic! Have you experienced political games at your workplace? Perhaps a co-worker tells a story to entice you to act when it isn't 100 percent truthful. What do you do?

Watch what Nehemiah did.

He kept working. He continued until the wall was complete.

Nehemiah never took his focus from God's purpose. Regardless how hard his enemies tried; Nehemiah did not lose focus. He wasn't tempted to meet with his enemies even to quiet them. He didn't fall into the temptation of distraction. He worked on his mission.

HOW TO AVOID CO-WORKERS DISTRACTIONS

- Don't give in to the temptation of a co-worker's story. Stay focused on the task and goal.
- Ask questions before you "take the bait" from a co-worker.
- Ask questions to validate and verify where they learned the information and to determine their motivation.

Nehemiah's accomplishments through the practice of focusing

No one has the exact dimensions of Jerusalem's wall, but estimates indicate it was approximately 13,200 feet around the city with an average height of 40 feet and approximately 8 feet thick.[6] The wall was partially destroyed and severely damaged. In some sections, it needed to be rebuilt completely. Nehemiah and his team rebuilt it in *fifty-two days*.

Comparison to the Colosseum and Hadrian's Wall

To put Nehemiah's accomplishments into perspective, let's compare his efforts with the Roman Colosseum and Hadrian's Wall in England.

The Roman Colosseum was built in six to eight *years*. It was 620 feet long and 164 feet high.[7] The emperor Vespasian ordered the building of the amphitheater in 70 A.D. after the siege of Jerusalem.[8] It was paid for by the treasures stolen from Jerusalem along with an estimated 100,000 Jewish prisoners.[28] Nehemiah's team took fifty-two *days* to rebuild a wall that was 13,200 feet around the city with an average height of 40 feet.

England's Hadrian's Wall is 36,960 feet long, took six years to build, and was built by approximately 15,000 men.[9]

It took Nehemiah and approximately forty-four workers fifty-two days to build 13,200 feet of wall. The Bible documents that forty-four workers and teams of people helped in the reconstruction efforts. It isn't specific on the total number, but it's doubtful there were as many as who built the Colosseum or Hadrian's Wall.

The art of focus and prioritization

Nehemiah accomplished his mission in record time. Focus and prioritization create a sense of accomplishment because projects and programs *are finished*. The sense of accomplishment changes attitudes toward the workday and increases productivity and engagement. Practicing focus and prioritization provides clarity to the chaos.

THE ART OF FOCUS AND PRIORITIZATION

How to prioritize tasks, projects, and activities between multiple requests.

- First, determine who is the person making the request. Are they the boss? If yes, then prioritize it based on their expectations.
- Second, evaluate the request against current priorities and mission for the company. Is it aligned with the goals and mission of the department and of the organization?
- If the requester doesn't offer a deadline, suggest one. Most people, even the boss, understand the power of prioritization. Suggesting the due date keeps you in control of your schedule.
- Here's a tip from a mentor of mine: He said, "Melissa, someone else's emergency doesn't make it *your* emergency." Keep this in mind as you negotiate the due date.
- Once the assignment is accepted, communicate status updates continuously. Constant communication builds trust and confidence in your abilities.

Nehemiah taught us two lessons:

1. Focus on God for guidance, and
2. Focus on the mission

> Use the art of prioritization to align daily activities with the goals and mission.
> When distraction appears and others try to deter you from His purpose, quote Nehemiah, *"I am carrying on a great project and cannot go down."*

Temptation: Pride & ego

But He gives us more grace. That is why Scripture says:

"God opposes the proud but gives grace to the humble." James 4:6

How do pride and ego fit into temptation? Pride and ego may interfere with doing God's work or with relationships.

Ego leadership

Ego leadership is a leadership style that focuses on the leader and not on the team. It's the opposite of servant leadership. Decisions are made based on advancing the self-importance of the leader and improving their reputation.

Have you been led by someone who leads with ego leadership? Do *you* lead with ego leadership? This section builds on lesson three's discussion on ego leadership.

Leaders who lead with ego leadership begin their decision-making process with the question: How will this decision impact me, my job, my status, or my future?

This sounds harsh but, in many cases, it's true.

Some may think leaders who focus on themselves are focused on promotions and climbing the corporate ladder, and they don't care about others.

This isn't necessarily true.

They do care about others and do good for the company *if* it benefits them. They may volunteer to organize a charitable event or fundraiser which gives them personal recognition.

The personal recognition [ego] drives the decision to volunteer and not the mission of the charitable event.

Ego leadership at work

Can you think of someone who leads with an ego leadership style? If so, what frustrates you? Have you accepted their leadership style? Are you aware it's their leadership style?

In some cases, the ego leadership style is obvious, and the relationship may be toxic. Soon, either the leader leaves the company or other employees leave. A typical response from the employees is to ignore the leader and go about their business.

How to identify ego leadership

First, have patience with the situation and the person. Evaluate the person's leadership style to be sure it's truly ego leadership. Everyone has a story, and it's possible this person's story influenced their leadership style and personality.

Use Grace & Salt communication skills to uncover their story and break through their outer shell. The goal is to make a new friend by sincerely trying to understand the person.

This sounds easy, but it's actually very difficult. It's difficult because of your own ego.

I'm asking you to put your feelings and ambition to the side while you evaluate another. I'm asking you to adopt a servant leadership mindset until you know if this person demonstrates ego leadership.

Is ego leadership my style?

Ego may interfere with the leader's impact. Don't misunderstand. Being focused on your "personal brand" is important. Taking actions to promote your brand and identify as a leader are necessary. However, allowing ego to interfere may hurt relationships at work or at home.

ACTIVITY: EGO LEADERSHIP STYLE: DO YOU LEAD WITH EGO LEADERSHIP?

This exercise identifies if decisions lean toward your benefit or the benefit of others. Identify a decision you made that involved a direct employee. If you don't have direct employees, think of a decision that involved others in your organization.
Ask these questions: (Be honest. No one will see the responses.)

1. Was the customer the focal point in the decision-making process?
2. Was the decision made to advance your career?
3. (If applicable) Was the impact to the employee considered in the decision-making process? Would the decision impact them or their career?
4. On a scale of 1 to 5, with 1 being never and 5 being always, how often do you make leadership decisions based on your personal career goals?

Take time to think about your actions and decisions. If you aren't sure, keep track of your decisions in a journal. Most don't think ego drives decisions, but my guess is you'll see ego plays a bigger part than you think.

Self-Reflection

Self-reflection is critical to becoming a better leader as well as understanding the power and responsibility leaders hold. One way to ensure that pride and ego stay under control is to verify the motivations behind the decisions.

Follow the Customer-Company question technique.

HOW TO KEEP PRIDE AND EGO UNDER CONTROL IN DECISION MAKING

Customer-Company Question Technique
1. During the decision-making process, ask these questions in order:
   "Is it good for the customer?"
   "Is it good for the company?"
2. If the answer is "yes" to either question, then ego is not driving the decision.
3. If the answer is "no", then ego may be playing a part in the decision.

Reflect on the decision and determine if a better decision is available that is good for the customer *and* the company.

This technique brings perspective to the situation and makes the decision-making process easier. If it's not good for the customer or the company, then there must be a better decision.

How does ego leadership interfere with decisions?

Imagine your company is experiencing a downturn in sales and considers reducing budgets and employees. You're a member of the executive team and was promoted to vice president. Your plan is to become president.

"That's odd. John called an emergency meeting for the executive team first thing tomorrow morning." *John hasn't been president long and typically doesn't call emergency meetings. I wonder what's going on.*

It's quiet and somber as we sit around the board table nervously waiting for John to speak.

"Okay, we're all here. What's going on?" Joe asks.

"I had a call last night with the corporate office on our financial performance. You all know we've missed projections for three months in a row and haven't shown a good plan to mitigate the shortfall before the end of the year. So, I'm sure everyone knows what's next. Budget cuts, and if we don't meet the number, it will be people too."

There are two choices to overcome a business plan shortfall: (1) increase sales and (2) cut costs. It's that simple and that difficult.

"Okay. You know the drill. Jaime, rework the sales plan, call customers, and talk to marketing on special promotions we can launch."

"We all need to look at budgets and complete an organizational evaluation to understand each employee's value. Look at every job and its function. Is it necessary? Are there employees that duplicate activities or can absorb additional responsibilities? Should we combine departments?

"If we have employees with poor performance, consider them, as well. HR can direct you if you have questions. Basically, how do we meet our goals and reduce the head count?

"As far as budgets go, cut costs or delay programs and purchases to next year. I know this is tough, but it has to be done. Let's see. Today's Wednesday. Let's meet Friday morning to review."

Really? Do I have to do this? Is this what it's like to be a member of the executive team? I understand finding sales and launching marketing programs.

But, laying off people? If I'm not careful, I'll have a heart attack. My heart is racing, and I can't breathe. I better find sales and cut costs so we don't have to cut people.

Looking at each other, we quietly walk out of the office.

I clear my calendar and put everything on hold. This is my top priority. Before I do anything, I need to communicate to my team members. This is an "all hands-on-deck" situation, and everyone must find dollars to cut.

But I don't want to cause panic either. They're going to know what's next: a layoff.

"Hi, Sophia. This is Jaimie. Do you have a few minutes? Would you come to my office and ask Nick to join you? Thanks."

Sophia and Nick walk in and sit down at my conference table.

"Thanks for coming down so quickly. Well, as you know, we haven't met our sales goals for the past several months so, it's that time again. Time to find budget dollars to cut."

"Sophia, dig into both the sales and marketing budgets. Any projects and programs that we haven't paid, delay them until next year. I'll need a detailed report by Thursday afternoon with the total dollars cut, by month, per line item. Sorry for the last minute notice, but I'm sure you understand the pressure we're under."

"Nick, I want you to focus on sales opportunities and possible marketing campaigns to drive sales. Again, I'll need a detailed list of sales opportunities by dollar value, account name, and timing. Get your team moving on this immediately."

"Thanks, guys. If you have any questions, call or text me. That's it."

Now, it's my turn. The organization.

I print off the organizational charts by department and begin an in-depth evaluation.

Can employees be reassigned to different roles or departments? Where is there duplication? What about the parts department? The people who enter parts orders do the same job as the people who enter the equipment orders. Right?

Department by department, I look at each role and determine if there is duplication in the activities or if they are necessary to meet our goals.

Man, this is tough, but it's my defining moment. If I want to be president, these are the tough choices I'll need to make.

How do I keep ego out of the decisions? Everyone else is looking at their organization too. What if proposals overlap and someone else proposes a restructure plan where they combine departments giving another executive more responsibility and remove it from mine?

I need to ask two questions. "Is it good for the customer, and is it good for the company?" These questions help me stay focused and keep my ego and personal advancement plan out of the decision making.

Whew! It's finished and on time.

It's Friday, and I'm ready to present my proposal to the team.

We go around the table, and each person presents their organization evaluation and budget cuts. It's my turn.

My strategy is to begin with the budget cuts just in case the proposed cuts equal the dollars needed and no employees are impacted.

"This is great progress, but we'll need more. What suggestions do you have for head count reduction?" John asks.

No such luck.

I review the reorganization plan which is accepted by the team. Everyone agrees to move forward with both the budget cuts and the restructuring plan.

Back in my office, I take a deep breath. *Good job presenting a well-thought-out plan.* I'm proud of myself for the courage it took to make those decisions. But I'm so sorry for the employees that will be impacted.

Now, it's time to tell the staff. I don't want them to hear it from the rumor mill.

Well, I think that went well. Everyone seemed to understand.

My telephone rings. "Hello?"

"Hi, Jaime. It's Sharon. Hey, um, thank you for telling everyone about the restructuring plans. Um. But a lot of the employees are getting nervous. They think you didn't share everything and that you're hiding something. Well, I thought you should know."

What? What happened? I thought I communicated clearly and completely. What did I say or do that would lead them to think I was not being 100% truthful?

"Thanks for telling me, Sharon. I'll think through the next steps."

After talking with the employees individually, I found that no matter how good, clear, and frequent the communication was, there was more to be shared. I underestimated the affect these changes had on the employees.

After all, I told employees they'd be moving to different departments, changing job roles, and reporting to different bosses. I upset their lives.

Situation assessment

After reviewing the decision and the employee feedback, I asked myself if pride was involved with the decisions and strategy.

Did I move through the implementation plan because I developed the strategy? Could I have explained the intent behind the changes more clearly or earlier to help ease the transition? What could I have done differently to help the employees understand the purpose of the reorganization?

Yes, I could have done all of that and more.

Make business personal

The following scene is from *You've Got Mail*.

This is the scene where Meg Ryan's character (Kathleen Kelly) is sick, and Tom Hanks's character (Joe Fox) comes to her apartment to cheer her up. He explains that moving his business, Fox Books, into her neighborhood is strictly business and isn't personal.

"It's not personal. It's business," he says.

She replies, "What is that supposed to mean? I'm so sick of that. All it means is that it wasn't personal to you, but it was personal to me. It's personal to a lot of people. But what's so wrong with being personal anyway? Because whatever else anything is, it ought to begin by being personal."[10]

This message from Kathleen Kelly is critical. Business should be personal.

In the above example, Jaime should have considered the impact on the employees and incorporated "being personal" into his communication plans.

DURING YOUR NEXT MEETING OR INTERACTION WITH AN EMPLOYEE OR CO-WORKER, REMEMBER YOU ARE SPEAKING TO A PERSON—A PERSON WITH BOTH PERSONAL AND PROFESSIONAL WORRIES AND STRESSES. THE DECISION MAY NOT CHANGE BUT THE APPROACH SHOULD.

TIPS ON KEEPING BUSINESS PERSONAL

- Listen with grace. Everyone has a story.
- Listen to understand. Use active listening techniques. Don't determine the response before they finish their thought.
- Fill the message with grace *and salt* [truth]. Don't sugarcoat the message. Be clear.
- Anticipate the personal nature of the discussion. How will they respond?
- Anticipate their thoughts and anxiety toward the changes or message. If it's a role change, anticipate their concern for what others will think of the change. Will they be concerned with their reputation? Will they want the new role?
- Communicate the reason behind the discussion or changes from a frame of reference they would understand.
- Acknowledge the anxiety or feelings toward the changes. Listen and hear them.
- Prepare by putting yourself in their shoes or situation.
- Allow time for the employee to process the changes and ask questions.
- Follow-up with the employee a day or two after the meeting to be sure their questions have been answered. Sometimes questions arise after the moment has passed.

LESSON VII: TEMPTATION: PRIDE & EGO -
KEEP PRIDE AND EGO UNDER CONTROL.
FOCUS ON SERVANT LEADERSHIP AND RECOGNIZE
WHEN EGO LEADERSHIP BEGINS TO CONTROL DECISIONS.

DECISION-MAKING TEST TO REMOVE EGO:

Is it good for the customer?
Is it good for the company?
And remember: Business should be personal.
Reference "Tips on keeping business personal" in daily conversations.

LESSON VIII: COURAGE — BE LIKE ESTHER: STAND UP, SPEAK UP, AND STEP OUT

He sent back this answer: "Do not think that because you are in the king's house you alone of all the Jews will escape. For if you remain silent at this time, relief and deliverance for the Jews will arise from another place, but you and your father's family will perish. And who knows but that you have come to royal position for such a time as this?"
Esther 4:13-14

*E*sther was a beautiful, young Jewish woman and Mordecai's niece. It's estimated that she was fourteen when she became queen of Persia.[1] After the king divorced Queen Vashti over an indiscretion, he searched for a new queen and chose Esther as his new bride and queen.

Her uncle, Mordecai, became her caregiver early in her life. Concerned for her safety, he told her not to tell anyone, including the king, she was Jewish.

Mordecai and Esther earn King Xerxes' trust

One day, Mordecai sits at the palace gates, where he learns of a plot against the king. Mordecai tells Esther about the plot, and Esther tells the king. After an investigation, two guards were put to death. Because Esther and Mordecai told the king of the plot, they gained his trust.

King Xerxes agrees with Haman's plan

Uncovering the plot made the king nervous for his safety so he promotes Haman to the highest royal position above all nobles. With this position, everyone in the kingdom must bow to Haman. However, Mordecai refuses. Haman becomes angry and develops a plot to kill Mordecai and all of the Jews.

Haman convinces King Xerxes that there are people in his kingdom who don't honor their culture and traditions and should be punished. One way to remove these people is to destroy them. The king blindly agrees and makes the decree.

King Xerxes doesn't know Queen Esther's ancestry. It's time for Esther to tell the king the truth. Mordecai instructs her to tell the king that she is Jewish. The king's decree would include putting her to death and all of her people.

Esther approaches the king

The only way to speak with the king is if you are summoned by him. Esther needs the "favor" or a summons to speak with the king. She's petrified. What if the king doesn't summon her?

Mordecai reminds her, *"Do not think that because you are in the king's house you alone of all the Jews will escape. For if you remain silent at this time, relief and deliverance for the Jews will arise from another place, but you and your father's family will perish. And who knows but that you have come to royal position for such a time as this?"* Esther 4:13-14

She tells Mordecai to gather the Jews and fast for three days. She'd do the same. At the end of three days, she'd go to the king and *"...if I perish, I perish."* Esther 4:16

She puts on her royal robes and goes to the courtyard. If the king doesn't hold out his golden scepter to her, she'd be put to death.

Think about that.

Imagine how scared she is. She's fourteen years old and knows she will die if the king doesn't hold out his scepter to her. She courageously steps out in faith and risks her life to save thousands of Jewish people.

The good news is that the king raises his scepter and accepts her into his throne room.

Esther's dilemma

It's difficult to understand the dilemma Esther faced. She was raised in poverty and early in life was brought into the king's harem. She was showered with makeup, perfume, and clothes made of silk and beautiful designs. She became queen.

The strength and courage she demonstrated to risk her comfortable life and potential death to stand up against what she knew was wrong is unfathomable. She could have ignored Mordecai and continued to eat good food, bathe in perfumed bathwater, and wear beautiful silk robes, but instead, she chose to do the right thing and go to the king unsummoned.

Esther risked her life by going to the king without his permission or request. Haman was eventually hanged, saving the Jewish people.

Esther's story is an example of how we could step out of our comfort zone and take a risk at home, in our community, and at work. Take a few minutes and read the book of Esther. If you don't have a Bible, go to www.biblegateway.com.

Stepping out in faith scenario

It's been ten years and time for a change.

Man, am I bored. I like my job, but I have more to offer. I want to become a key account manager and work with the Latin American distributors.

Well, it's now or never.

Walking into my boss's office, I say, "Hi, Jeremy. Do you have a moment? I'd like to talk to you about a new role."

"Sure, what's on your mind?"

"What do you think about moving me to a Latin American key account manager role? I want to add more value to the organization and believe this is where I could help. What do you think?"

"Interesting idea. I'll run it by Greg and Steve and get back to you."

"Sounds good. Here is the presentation on how this move will impact the company."

"Great. I'll get back with you as soon as possible."

A few weeks later and I'm starting to wonder about his answer.

What if he says no?

Finally, he calls me into his office. "Well, thank you for your presentation and identifying additional ways you could positively impact the organization. But, we have a different idea. Would you be interested in joining the domestic sales team?"

What? Domestic? Hopefully my facial expression doesn't show my shock and surprise.

"Um. Domestic? Why Domestic? I speak Spanish, and the international market is all I know."

"Yes, that's true. But thinking about your future growth in the company, you'll need to gain the respect and knowledge of the domestic business. Moving to the domestic side will not only help the company but will help you long term."

"Let me think about it. I'll get back with you shortly. Thank you for considering me."

I thought about it, prayed, discussed it with my husband, and decided to take the risk. This was one of the hardest decisions I made in my career up to that point.

I call Jeremy and accept the position.

(Note: this scenario is true, but I paraphrased the conversation.)

The valley

I knew it would be a difficult transition, but what I didn't anticipate was that I'd feel like I didn't belong. I was the only woman on the sales team, and there weren't any women owners in the distributor organization.

For five years, my work life was lonely. I called it one of the "valley" times in my life. To start over and build my reputation with a new group of people was difficult and challenging. The domestic distributors and customers didn't know me. But using my abilities and integrity, I persevered and gained their trust.

The missing piece was a sense of belonging. Have there been times in your life where you didn't belong?

Think about Esther on her first day in the harem. The older women probably were jealous of her and didn't treat her kindly. She may have sat in the corner and watched the ladies interact. She didn't know the customs, how to dress, proper royal etiquette, or even what was expected of her. My guess is she was lonely.

Two Choices in the Valley

There are two choices when you're in the "valley" and lonely. The first is to stay where you are, go through the motions, and not make a difference. And the second is to have courage, like Esther, and step *into* the situation to make a change.

At my lowest point, I wanted to give up. Returning to my comfort zone was appealing. In the comfort zone, I felt valued and respected.

Courage to lead change

During a heart-to-heart conversation with a friend and mentor where I admitted the frustrations of being in a male-dominated network and hitting brick walls everywhere, he said, "Melissa, maybe you are where you are to bring a difference to the domestic side of the business."

"Really? You think so?"

Okay, maybe he's right. Sounds like Mordecai's message to Esther, doesn't it? *"And who knows but that you have come to royal position for such a time as this?"* Esther 4:14

Obviously, Esther's situation was graver and more serious, but the message is the same. Perhaps I was in the new role to make a difference. It was my responsibility to implement change regardless of the difficulties, challenges, and loneliness.

Reinvention

Plowing back into the mission and holding my head up with high standards and expectations, the sense of belonging finally returned. It wasn't easy but it was worth it.

Growth comes from discomfort. If I would have returned to my comfort zone and didn't push through the discomfort, growth would have been halted.

I draw on this experience and advice when in the discomfort zone. My friend and mentor passed away many years ago due to a long illness. To continue his legacy, I'm sharing his advice with you.

Esther's courageous character

What courageous moment have you avoided? What is a courageous moment? It doesn't have to be a situation where you're meeting with the president of your company or with an executive of a large corporation. It could be as simple as walking into a meeting and not knowing anyone. Or speaking up for a cause or in support of someone. Stepping out into the unknown and taking a risk by accepting a new position at work or in a community group.

BE COURAGEOUS!
BE LIKE ESTHER!

When facing a courageous moment, think of Esther.

ACTIVITY: BUILD A COURAGEOUS LEADERSHIP STYLE

Regardless of your role in an organization, fear dictates our behavior from time to time. This activity helps to overcome fear and push us into the discomfort zone.

Journal Prompt: (Download the journal page at www.graceandsaltbook.org/resources.)

What courageous moments face you today?

1. Identify one courageous moment that you will act upon in the next 24 hours.
2. Use the Grace and Salt log sheet or Grace and Salt journal to record the courageous moment and the outcome.
3. Repeat steps 1 and 2 to build a courageous leadership style.

The following scripture verses provide strength during courageous moments. Read them when fear creeps into your thoughts.

David also said to Solomon his son, "Be strong and courageous, and do the work. Do not be afraid or discouraged, for the LORD God, my God, is with you. He will not fail you or forsake you until all the work for the service of the temple of the LORD is finished." 1 Chronicles 28:20

When I am afraid, I put my trust in you. In God, whose word I praise, in God I trust; I will not be afraid. What can a mortal man do to me? Psalm 56:3-4

I can do everything through him who gives me strength. Philippians 4:13

Lesson VIII: Courage: Be Like Esther: Stand Up, Speak Up and Step Out

He sent back this answer: "Do not think that because you are in the king's house you alone of all the Jews will escape. For if you remain silent at this time, relief and deliverance for the Jews will arise from another place, but you and your father's family will perish. And who knows but that you have come to royal position for such a time as this?"
Esther 4:13-14

> Staying in your comfort zone is easy.
> Having the courage to stand up, speak up, and step out into the discomfort zone is where you'll grow.

LESSON IX: REFRESH YOURSELF — HAVE A SPA (SPIRITUAL PERSONAL ACTIVITY) DAY!

*Then, because so many people were coming and going
that they did not even have a chance to eat, he said to them,
"Come with me by yourselves to a quiet place and get some rest."*
Mark 6:31

Rest, refresh, and rejuvenate yourself through a Spiritual Personal Activity.

We're all busy, no matter the season of life. And finding rest is essential to your health and well-being.

But how do you do that?

How do you find rest when life is coming at you from all directions?

The answer is to be intentional and schedule rest-filled activities.

These look different to everyone. The next exercise identifies your personal rest-filled activities.

ACTIVITY: IDENTIFY REST-FILLED ACTIVITIES

Download the journal page from www.graceandsaltbook.com or open the Grace & Salt journal for this exercise.

1. Define the term "rest". What does it mean to you? When you think about resting and rejuvenating, what comes to mind?
2. Brainstorm for 3 minutes on what "rest" means to you.
3. Continue to brainstorm for 3 additional minutes on activities that would give you "rest" based on your definition.
4. Review the list of "rest" activities and circle the activities that are feasible. For example: Going to the beach gives you rest but might not be feasible. Taking a walk along a nearby lake is feasible.
5. Schedule the "rest" activities in your calendar. Do not cancel them or ignore them. Treat them as if your life depends on it because it does.

While in Spain writing this book, I took the time to wander and get lost. Traveling from Marbella to the tip of Spain, in and out of small towns enjoying the sunshine, hot weather, and God's beauty. Stopping in seaside towns to buy a bocadillo (sandwich) and sit on the rocks above the sea was incredibly restful.

I could literally feel the stress drain from me as the waves crashed along the shoreline when I dipped my toes in the chilly water.

The thoughts of these special memories help me relax and rest.

Let the guilt go

Removing yourself from the daily obligations is tough but required. And guilt may enter the picture when you try to "get away."

Will my spouse or partner understand if I take a few days to myself?

Will my team or my boss understand the decision to take a few vacation days? Will they leave me alone?

Will I forgive myself for taking time to refresh? Can I relax while I'm gone?

Bring God along

Life will always be crazy. It will look different, but craziness will always be present. To manage through it, take a few days or hours to walk *outside* of the craziness and walk *into* solitude. Go off the grid.

Traveling to faraway places isn't necessary. It's as easy as getting a massage or pedicure or taking a walk in a park. Go kayaking or spend time in nature and with nature.

The most important aspect of refueling and refreshing is to invite God along.

Begin with prayer. Open your mind. Let Him come into your heart. Read the Bible and listen deeply. Connecting with God is critical to your spiritual maturity and your sanity. It helps find clarity, focus, and purpose. The rest of life is just noise.

Billy Graham says it best. "Nothing can calm our souls more or better prepare us for life's challenges than time spent alone with God."[1]

Leaders need rest

Everyone demands moments of the leader's time. Employees are constantly looking for answers, wanting validation of their decisions, or wanting the leader to make the decision.

In Mark, Jesus drives out an impure spirit. He heals Simon's mother-in-law, who was sick with a fever. Later that evening, people brought all of the sick and demon-possessed. It's written that the *entire town* was at His door, and Jesus healed many with various diseases. People sought him out after hearing the stories from those healed. One person told another and another and so on and so on. Everyone wanted a piece of Him.

Jesus heals a desperate woman

Matthew 9:20-21 says, "Just then a woman who had been subject to bleeding for twelve years came up behind him and touched the edge of his cloak. She said to herself, 'If I only touch his cloak, I will be healed.'"

Jesus walks through the streets with people crowded around Him, and they push and pull to get a view of Him or to speak with Him. They knew His power and wanted Him to heal themselves or their family members. One woman knew that if she could just touch His cloak, she would be healed.

Can you imagine her desperation? She sees the crowd and knows of Jesus's reputation. She believes this is her one chance to stop the agony of the last twelve years. This scene reminds me of a concert or sporting event with general admission seating. Hundreds and thousands of people trying to get into the stadium to get the best seat.

This is the image that comes to mind when I think of this woman. She's pushing and moving through the crowd as quickly as possible to get to Jesus. Stretching her hand out as far as it will go to touch His robe. Her fingertips are so close...

The importance of rest from Jesus's perspective

Let's look at this from Jesus's perspective.

Imagine His stress with everyone around Him pushing and shoving, the disciples not always believing and questioning His words, and the hundreds and thousands of people wanting attention.

The street is packed with people with Jesus in the middle. They move like one unit down the street. He's jostled from one side to the other. People trying to get closer and closer to Him. One woman pushes through the crowd, and the crowd noise is too loud to hear her.

How overwhelming!

"Go away!" "Leave me alone." "Figure things out by yourself."

Isn't that what you'd have said? Crowds make me nervous.

She finally reaches Him and touches His cloak, and immediately she's healed.

This story has been used many times to illustrate different points, such as her faith in Jesus, her persistence, Jesus's power, and more.

We're focusing on the craziness in Jesus's life which may be how you're feeling right now.

But Jesus teaches us how to deal with the whirlwind of life. He refueled and rejuvenated through rest, prayer, and solitude with God.

Biblical reminders of the importance of rest

The Bible provides examples of Jesus resting through prayer. He sought solitude in quiet lonely places and rose early to walk up the mountainside to be alone and pray.

After he had dismissed them [the crowd]; he went up on a mountainside by himself to pray. Matthew 14:23

Again, He's seeking solitude to be with God.

Very early in the morning, while it was still dark, Jesus got up, left the house and went off to a solitary place, where he prayed. Mark 1:35

Exhausted, Jesus got up in the middle of the night or early morning to rest in prayer. He went to a solitary place to be alone with God.

But Jesus often withdrew to lonely places and prayed. Luke 5:16

One of those days Jesus went out to a mountainside to pray, and spent the night praying to God. Luke 6:12

Now it's your turn.

Let's identify two restful activities that allow you to rejuvenate.

ACTIVITY: CHOOSE & COMMIT TO TWO REST-FILLED ACTIVITIES

1. Choose two rest-filled activities from the Rest-filled Activities worksheet completed earlier.

Rest-filled Activity #1 _____

_____

Rest-filled Activity #2 _____

_____

2. Schedule them in your calendar as critical appointments.
3. Find an accountability buddy and tell them your two rest-filled activities and schedule.

Rest-filled activities are difficult for me. Breaks are rare and need to be scheduled. I've identified two rest-filled activities to share.

1. Walk around the block (weather permitting) or on the treadmill twice each day for fifteen minutes.
2. Read a book for fifteen minutes once per day, three times per week.

The first rest-filled activity gets me out of my chair, and the second focuses my mind away from the computer.

Since I've told you my plans, you are now my accountability buddy. Please send me a note to see how I'm doing. My email address is melissa@graceandsaltbook.com. I'd love to hear from you, and I expect you to share with me your rest-filled activities.

Lesson XII: Refresh Yourself – Have a SPA (Spiritual Personal Activity) Day!

Then, because so many people were coming and going that they did not even have a chance to eat, he said to them, "Come with me by yourselves to a quiet place and get some rest." Mark 6:31

> Life will always be crazy. It will look different, but craziness will always be present. To manage it, take a few days or hours to walk *outside* of the craziness and walk *into* solitude. Go off the grid.

LESSON X: SELF-AWARENESS & GROWTH — THE NEW YOU

...make every effort to add to your faith goodness; and to goodness, knowledge; and to knowledge, self-control; and to self-control, perseverance; and to perseverance, godliness; and to godliness, mutual affection; and to mutual affection, love. For if you possess these qualities in increasing measure, they will keep you from being ineffective and unproductive in your knowledge of our Lord Jesus Christ.[1]
2 Peter 1:5-8

Self-awareness and growth. Where are you in your leadership development journey?

To answer that question, let's explore the metrics. Who do you measure against? And how do you measure where you are in your development?

The benchmark

In all measurement activities, a benchmark is required. Who is the benchmark to compare our development? What are the attributes and characteristics they possess? You might guess that Jesus is the benchmark.

Have you heard the saying "What would Jesus do?" This saying was born from the concept of becoming more like Jesus. He is the benchmark of our comparison and evaluation. To become more like Jesus, it's necessary to understand His attributes and characteristics.

There are three steps we'll review:

1. Jesus's leadership attributes
2. Identify our baseline, and
3. Identify two areas to focus upon in the next ninety days

Step 1: Jesus's leadership characteristics

Who is Jesus and what attributes does He instruct us to develop?

I studied the gospels of Matthew, Mark, Luke, and John and compared them to determine Jesus's leadership attributes. The four books provided consistent descriptions of Jesus's leadership style.

To identify a comprehensive picture of Jesus's leadership style, I combined both His teachings and His attributes.

Below, you'll find a list of Jesus' attributes followed by a list of his corresponding teachings.

The Bible verses are included for easy reference to conduct your own research. Take time to read the verses, rather than reading Jesus's teachings and leadership attributes as listed.

Reading the verses in context helps to understand how the Bible verse connects to the teaching. There are others that apply, and you may disagree with my evaluation.

Dig into the book of Matthew. You'll be glad you did.

Jesus' teachings according to Matthew

JESUS' ATTRIBUTES

- Compassionate & generous.
- Focused on God – alignment.
- Humble & quiet.
- Evangelist.
- Love & be kind to everyone.
- Prayerful.
- Trust in God.
- Servant leader.
- Forgiving.
- Honesty before all else.
- Integrity.

- Compassion (Matthew 4:23)
- Light of the world (Matthew 5:14)
- Reconcile relationships and settle matters quickly (Matthew 5:23)
- Integrity – Keep oaths and promises (Matthew 5:33)
- Generosity (Matthew 5:38-42)
- Love everyone, even the enemy (Matthew 5:43-48)
- Humility – Give to the needy (Matthew 6:1-4)
- Don't judge (Matthew 7:1-5)
- Treat others the way you want to be treated (Matthew 7:12)
- Trust in God – Give burdens to Him (Matthew 11:28)
- Sense of purpose – He shows why He came and why He must go (Matthew 16:21, 20:28)
- Strong convictions (Matthew 21:12-13)
- Love God with your heart, mind, and soul (Matthew 22:37)
- Time in solitude with God (Matthew 26: 36-45)
- Go and spread the Word through your actions, words, and works (Matthew 28:16-20)

Step 2: Baseline self-assessment

Conducting a baseline of where you're at currently in your development provides the metric for comparison.

This next step may be difficult and will take time to complete.

SELF-ASSESSMENT BASELINE PREPARATION INSTRUCTIONS

- Take a piece of paper or use the Grace & Salt journal.
- Find a quiet place.
- Open your mind.
- Begin with prayer and meditation to remove the world's stress from this time of reflection.
- Schedule assessment and reflection time in your calendar. Make this self-assessment a priority.
- Be honest with yourself. Self-assessments don't work if you aren't honest and open to the evaluation.
- Write your answers. Research shows that writing reinforces remembering concepts.
- Download the assessment at www.graceandsaltbook.com/resources or complete it below.

The self-assessment includes a definition of each attribute and specific questions to help you rate yourself.

Rate each attribute using the rating scale from 1 – 5 (1 = not at all and 5 = excellent). Don't overthink it. Use your best judgement on how you think you portray that specific attribute.

There are no wrong answers.

1. Compassionate and generous

This attribute references being compassionate and caring toward others, including strangers and people you don't like.

Do you reach out to neighbors to help with yard work (or a chore) without being asked? Are you generous with your money and donate to specific charities or organizations?

Besides money, are you donating time, energy, and knowledge to give back to the community? Are you generous with time and money when people aren't looking?

What about your behavior when driving? This is a good indication on your compassion. How do you respond when someone "cuts you off" or doesn't allow you to merge?

RATING: _____

2. Focused on God – spiritual alignment

Where are you spiritually? Active in mission work, church, community, Bible study? Think about your social network (online and in-person). If asked, what would others say about your faith? Would they know you are a Christian? Think about your actions at work, in the community, and with your family. Are your actions aligned with God's Word?

RATING: _____

3. Humble and quiet

Think about your listening skills. Would others consider you a good listener? Where do you put your priorities with God and others? Are you genuinely interested in what people say and their experiences, or are you thinking about yourself while they are talking? Look at your schedule. Where do you spend your time? This is a good indication of humility.

RATING: _____

4. Evangelist

Think about your conversations. How do you speak? What language (word choice) do you use? Would others consider you a Christian by your conversations?

What is your approach to evangelize? Relational: where you wait for the opportunity to approach the topic. Relentless: where you dive in even if the other person isn't ready to hear the message.

How do others respond to your message and approach? Should it be altered? Do you speak boldly in the workplace, community, and at church? Think about your level of courage. According to Jesus, our main purpose in life is to make disciples who make disciples.

RATING: _____

5. Love and be kind to everyone

Think about your love for everyone, even your enemies. Enemies to you, your family, at work, or against the country. Are you showing love to everyone you meet? Are you kind and respectful? Think about your patience level (use the driving example).

RATING: _____

6. Prayerful

Think about your prayer life. What does your prayer life look like? Think about the amount of time you're spending in prayer. Are your prayers one-sided discussions, or do you sit and wait to hear God's voice? What type of prayers do you say? Who and what is included in your prayers? How much time is dedicated to prayer?

RATING: _____

7. Trust in God (and Jesus)

How much do you trust God will provide in a crisis? Have there been times when your trust level was low and you wanted to control the situation? Think through where you are on the "trust in God" scale. We can always trust Him more than we do today even though He doesn't always provide in ways we want. Many times, we won't see His plan until we're through it. Where are you on the scale of trusting in God?

RATING: _____

8. Servant leader

The leader is a servant to their team. Supporting them during a crisis. Removing obstacles so that they complete their tasks. It's the opposite of an autocratic boss, dictator, or micromanager.

Think about your leadership style. What would your team say about your style if asked? Would they consider your style autocratic and micromanaging? Would they consider your style participatory and collaborative? Do you exhibit servant leadership characteristics? Reference lesson IV for further details.

RATING: _____

9. Forgiving

Think about your relationships: family, friends, colleagues, neighbors, Facebook friends. How easy is it to forgive if someone posts an unflattering picture of you on social media? How would you handle the situation? How strong and full of trust are your family relationships? Reference forgiveness in Lesson VII. How easy is it for you to forgive yourself? Forgiveness is critical to growth.

RATING: _____

10. Honesty before all else – trustworthiness

Jesus mentions truth fifty-six times in the book of John. He says "I tell you the truth" twenty-seven times prior to making a statement or providing a message/lesson. Honesty and trust are important attributes of Jesus. Think about your honesty and trust rating. Does your team trust you? How do you know if you're trustworthy? Stephen Covey's (2006) book, *The Speed of Trust* outlines thirteen behaviors that build trust. Read this book if this is an area of improvement in your development.

RATING: _____

11. Integrity

Integrity goes hand in hand with trust. Where are you on the integrity rating? Are your values and ethics aligned with your actions? According to Covey (2006), integrity is "deep honesty and truthfulness. It is who we really are. It includes congruence, humility and courage." How strong is your integrity? Are you open and honest in your conversations? Do those around you know what you stand for? Think about your thoughts, words, and actions. Are they aligned? What would others say about you, if asked?

RATING: _____

Step 3: Identify two ratings

Review your ratings for each attribute. Identify two attributes rated below a three.

Step 4: Develop an improvement plan

The next step is to establish a development plan to improve these areas.

For example: I rated myself 2 on the prayerful attribute. I pray once a day on weekdays at home, but when I'm traveling, I don't pray at all. It's interesting that when I sit in the driver's seat of my car, I'm prompted to pray. When I'm traveling or in a hotel, it doesn't cross my mind. How am I going to remember to pray? What will I do to pray more often?

- Action 1: Schedule time to pray on my calendar. My calendar will send me an alert and reminder. Sounds silly? Maybe. However, it's an effective strategy to form a habit.
- Action 2: Journal during and after prayer. A prayer journal provides a record of the prayers *and* the answers. It's important to see God's work in our lives.
- Action 3: Establish the goal. The prayerful benchmark is three times per week. The goal is five times per week.
- Action 4: Determine a measurement tool. I'll log each time I pray to track prayerful progress.
- Action 5: Accountability. I'll tell my accountability partner of my goal and ask them to keep me accountable.

THE IMPROVEMENT PLAN STEPS ARE:

(1) identify two attributes to improve, (2) identify the measurements, (3) identify current benchmarks in each attribute, (4) identify your goal (improved measurement and time frame), and (5) tell an accountability partner.

Measurement

The improvement plan steps are self-explanatory except for measurement. Measurement is critical to understand your progress. We know to measure ourselves against Jesus's benchmark, but how do we measure our progress in the development plan? After all, why have a plan if you don't know if you're achieving it?

I'll use the example of my prayer life. I rated myself a 2 and established a benchmark to pray on average three times per week, and my goal is to pray five times per week.

How will I know if I'm meeting my goal and, better yet, how will I know if I'm falling back to old habits of three times per week or worse? The answer is through measurement. A downloadable version of the tracking sheet is located at www.graceandsaltbook.com/resources.

Once the goal is reached, continue to monitor. Prayer life is important to my development, so I continue to monitor my progress to ensure that I'm maintaining the goal and not returning to old habits.

Creating charts to provide a quick visual glance at your progress is another method to show weekly progress. Don't be afraid to share them with your accountability partner.

Accountability partner relationship

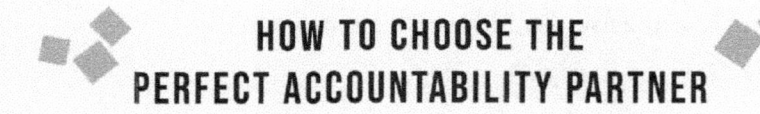

HOW TO CHOOSE THE PERFECT ACCOUNTABILITY PARTNER

- Choose someone you trust and can speak honestly to without fear of hurting the relationship.
- Choose someone who understands your development plans and the importance to improve in each area.
- Tell them your expectations of the relationship, i.e., honesty, consistent and open communication, that it's okay to ask about your progress, or push you if lack of progress exists, etc.
- Select a person who you would take shopping. The person who honestly answers the question, "Do I look fat in this dress?"
- Give them permission to reach out to you.
- Schedule time for accountability discussions.
- Share your successes and celebrations. It's more fun to celebrate with another person.
- Be an inspiration. Talk with them about their goals and if they are interested in learning more about the self-assessment.

LESSON X: SELF-AWARENESS AND GROWTH: THE NEW YOU

...make every effort to add to your faith goodness; and to goodness, knowledge; and to knowledge, self-control; and to self-control, perseverance; and to perseverance, godliness; and to godliness, mutual affection; and to mutual affection, love. For if you possess these qualities in increasing measure, they will keep you from being ineffective and unproductive in your knowledge of our Lord Jesus Christ.[2] 2 Peter 1:5-8

"What would Jesus do?"
This saying was born from the concept of becoming more like Jesus.
He is the benchmark of our comparison and evaluation.
To become more like Jesus, it's necessary to understand His attributes and characteristics.

LESSON XI: MENTOR - HAVE ONE, BE ONE

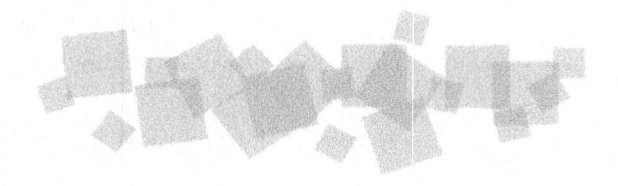

"Come, follow me," Jesus said, "and I will send you out to fish for people."[1]
Matthew 4:19

*M*entorship. Learning from others and giving to others are benefits to a mentor-mentee relationship. Mentorship is directly correlated to servant leadership. It's giving back by serving others to help their development and growth. Reaching a senior vice-president level would not have been possible without both professional and personal mentors.

In Matthew 4:19 Jesus instructs us to follow Him, and He will send us out to fish for people. Meaning, go make disciples [of Jesus] who will make disciples [of Jesus]. Taking this one step further, it means to mentor others while you disciple them.

The mentorship process teaches others to mentor or practice discipleship. It's a process that will change the world. Mentor programs have been attributed to increasing motivation and productivity along with potentially having a positive impact on burnout and overall positive job satisfaction[2].

The dictionary defines a mentor as a wise and trusted counselor or teacher[3]. Throughout the Bible, we're instructed to mentor others, to be a counselor and to listen to counsel.

Therefore, go and make disciples of all nations, baptizing them in the name of the Father and of the Son and of the Holy Spirit, and teaching them to obey everything I have commanded you. Matthew 28:19-20

And the things you have heard me say in the presence of many witnesses entrust to reliable men who will also be qualified to teach others. 2 Timothy 2:2

Instruct a wise man and he will be wiser still; teach a righteous man and he will add to his learning. Proverbs 9:9

For lack of guidance a nation falls, but many advisers make victory sure. Proverbs 11:14

The way of a fool seems right to him, but a wise man listens to advice. Proverbs 12:15

As iron sharpens iron so one man sharpens another (Proverbs 27:17) gets to the heart of mentorship and its importance. We sharpen each other to make each other better.

A mentor may help navigate office politics and challenges. They may provide assistance or listen to personal or professional questions or situations.

The relationship should be filled with trust, respect, and confidence. And, at times, it may evolve to mutual mentorships.

One mentor of mine began as a supplier. Through working together and building trust, we became friends, and he naturally became a mentor. He is a confidant, advisor, and trusted friend who has been with me every step of this journey for over twenty years.

Your mentor relationships may not develop into long-standing friendships and may be strictly professional. Mentor relationships come in all types and sizes.

Can you think about a time when you were overwhelmed or needed advice on a situation in your personal or professional life? Who did you reach out to? A family member? Friend? Colleague? Hopefully, there is someone in your life to talk to in times of stress and in times of joy.

The mentor relationship

There are two objectives for a mentor: to listen and to guide. The relationship between the mentee and mentor determines if one or both objectives apply.

The best mentorship relationships are those that are built on trust and genuine care for each other. They may include advice or discussions on dealing with conflict resolution or managing upward and downward in an organization.

Managing upward

Managing upward is managing your boss. This may sound strange, but to be a value to your boss, determine the best way to manage them —the best way to communicate and to anticipate their needs.

TIPS TO MANAGE THE BOSS

- Determine their preferred style of communication.
  - » Do they prefer: in-person, e-mail, text, or voice mail?
  - » How often do they want updates? Daily? Weekly? Never?
  - » What is their definition of an "emergency" or "crisis"?
- Determine their expectation of you and others. Ask them and observe them.
- Identify their leadership style.
- Identify their communication style.
- Incorporate the findings into your style when interacting with them.

Managing downward

Managing downward is managing direct employees or possibly managing employees in other departments that are lower on the organizational chart. For example, managing a cross-functional team where you are the leader and responsible for the team's performance.

How to be a mentor

ATTRIBUTES OF A MENTOR

- A generous listener.
- Shares experiences.
- Instills confidence.
- Provides gentle nudging.
- Not a direct counselor or imparts knowledge.
- Is intentional with the relationship and its goals.

The core of effective mentorship is an open, trusting relationship.[4]

"It [mentorship] is a generous gift of time that multiplies and often coalesces as a desire to mentor others. The mentoring relationship can and should be fluid, including learning how to be a better mentor. As a mentee or a mentor, we do not need to 'have it all together,' we only need a willingness to listen generously and honestly share our vulnerability with others."[5]

Isn't that powerful? What freedom to know that someone would help through listening and sharing experiences with no judgement. And that there is the opportunity to help others through the same process. The freedom is knowing that you aren't alone in this journey and we don't have to have it all together.

Employee development is a principal role for a leader, and when both parties are engaged and committed to a successful outcome, the reward is indescribable.

The importance of a safe environment

An example of a successful mentor-mentee relationship was an employee of mine who began in an entry-level position. Our relationship was safe and trust-filled. She shared her career goals and objectives with confidence knowing they were confidential. She not only *thought* they were confidential, she needed to *feel* the discussions were confidential and that it was a safe place to talk about anything.

A safe environment was created through the alignment of actions and words. Intent is one of the four cores of credibility.[6] Covey defines intent as "your fundamental motive or agenda and the behavior that follows."[7]

She understood that my intent was to listen and understand her goals so that we could establish a career plan together. The only way for her to share her professional goals with me was to feel safe. This safe environment was built on trust. Trust was built through communicating intent in every discussion.

Self-efficacy

One reason this relationship worked well was that she had high self-efficacy. Self-efficacy is the ability for one to believe in achieving one's goals. Those with high self-efficacy have a good understanding of themselves. They know their strengths and weaknesses and are willing to listen to feedback and incorporate the feedback into their development plan.

Speaking up

Speaking up is the best way to achieve professional goals.

If the mentee's goals are unknown or they don't know how to verbalize them, take time to help them identify their goals.

Once known, create a plan to achieve them.

Since we worked through her career and personal goals together, it was a priority to provide development training, exposure to specific experiences, and stretch assignments. When in discussions relating to open positions, decisions were made based on knowing her career goals.

Take a look at my career. My career began in 1987 in an entry-level position and worked into middle management in 1991. However, I didn't tell anyone my career goals until 2006. For fifteen years, I moved throughout middle management, never shattering or cracking the proverbial glass ceiling. The minute I told an influential person my goals, I shot up to senior vice president like a rocket. Well, it did take a lot of hard work and ten more years, but you get my point.

The other benefit of sharing your career goals is to determine if you and your boss are aligned. Perhaps your boss tells you that they don't agree with your plans. What do you do? By speaking up and sharing your goals, the boss and company's plans for you are revealed. These may not align with you at all. Rather than wasting many more years hoping your goals are realized, you can make a decision on staying in the organization or moving to another organization to achieve your goals.

Be intentional with the relationship. Ask your employees and mentees their goals. Be the boss and leader who *pulls* the next generation of leaders *up through* the organization.

A strong mentor uncovers the mentee's voice and helps them speak up.

THREE ATTRIBUTES OF A MENTOR-MENTEE RELATIONSHIP AND ENVIRONMENT

- Create a trust-filled relationship.
- Create an environment that is open to sharing the deepest dreams and struggles.
- Create a confidential and safe environment.

Formal or informal mentor programs

When searching for a mentee, be sure the person wants to be mentored. If the mentor/mentee relationship is forced, it probably won't be successful. Many companies have mentorship programs that formally match the mentor partners. Although formal mentor programs positively promote employee engagement and development, studies show that formal programs may do more harm than good.[8]

Informal mentor relationships where the partnerships are developed naturally have the best results. Inzer and Crawford (2005) state that "a formal mentoring program is beneficial if it promotes informal mentoring and involves good mentors."[9]

There is a difference between coaching and mentoring, but the process is the same. A connection is critical for both a coaching and mentoring relationship to be successful.

When the relationship is forced, the ultimate benefit diminishes.

Mentees are active participants

Being a mentee is not a passive role. Mentees are active participants in the relationship. Many times, employees want to grow and be promoted but aren't willing to be active in their development. If the mentee isn't willing to work on their development, talk to them about the concerns. It will be a waste of everyone's time if you open doors but the employee isn't willing to do the necessary work to walk through it.

Have this discussion at the beginning of the relationship, whether the program is formal or informal.

ACTIVITY: 4 STEPS TO FIND A MENTEE

STEP 1: Identify who in your network may need a mentor.
STEP 2: Write down names of possible mentees.
   Think about people who seek your advice personally or professionally.
   Has God put someone in your life that should be mentored?
   What do they ask you about?
   Who would benefit from your experience?
   Do you connect with them?
   Are you already mentoring someone informally?
STEP 3: Identify the potential mentee.
STEP 4: Contact the mentee to ask if they would be interested. If they aren't interested, go back to Step 2.

Preparations for a mentor relationship

As you prepare for a mentor relationship, include the following in your initial discussion:

- Identify and communicate the expectations of both parties.
- Determine the meeting schedule.
- Determine boundaries on accessibility. Can they call anytime of the day or night, or is it more structured contact?
- Communicate the preferred form of contact. Text, e-mail, telephone call, social media, etc.
- Determine the scope of the mentor relationship. Professional only? Are personal concerns acceptable?
- Discuss confidentiality. The relationship will dissolve if there isn't trust in confidentiality.

"Two are better than one, because they have a good return for their labor: If either of them falls down, one can help the other up. But pity anyone who falls and has no one to help them up."[10] Ecclesiastes 4:9-10

If you're interested in learning about Jesus as a mentor, visit:

http://www.licoc.org/bible-studies/next-steps/an-intimate-walk-with-jesus/14-jesus-the-perfect-mentor-pt2.

There is no time like the present. Contact the person you chose to mentor and start the discussion today.

Lesson XI: Mentor – Have One, Be One

"Come, follow me," Jesus said, "and I will send you out to fish for people."[11]
   Matthew 4:19

"Two are better than one, because they have a good return for their labor: If either of them falls down, one can help the other up."[12]
   Ecclesiastes 4:9-10:

As iron sharpens iron, so one man sharpens another.
   Proverbs 27:17

> The freedom is knowing that you aren't alone in this journey
> and that we don't have to have it all together.

LESSON XII: THE POWER OF PRAYER IN LEADERSHIP

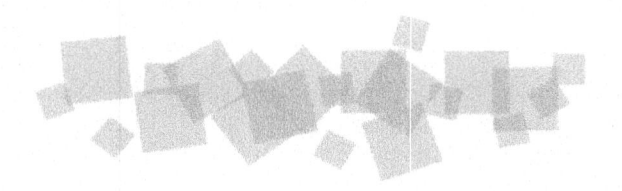

"Rejoice always, pray continually, give thanks in all circumstances; for this is God's will for you in Christ Jesus."
1 Thessalonians 5:16-18[1]

You've made it! We're on the last lesson in Grace & Salt. This lesson is the most important since we cannot speak enough about prayer.

I've dedicated two lessons, lessons VI and lesson XII, to prayer for good reason.

The first lesson focused on the armor of God and His protection as well as starting your day in prayer. Pray to understand God's will and listen to His instructions. Pray continually like Paul instructed in 1 Thessalonians 5:17.

In this lesson, lesson XII, we focus on the power of prayer in leadership and its impact on your life and the lives of others.

War Room

In 2015, the movie *War Room* was released. The main premise was to dedicate a room to prayer. A closet or a part of the bedroom is a suitable area. The size doesn't matter, but wherever it is, it's a place where the outside world doesn't enter literally and figuratively (thoughts).

A war room provides a dedicated space where prayer is the focus. Prayer for you and for others.

HOW TO CREATE A WAR ROOM

- Find a room or corner to dedicate to prayer. If a room or wall isn't available, use the top of a desk or table.
- Find paper or sticky notes to use as prayer notes.
- Write the prayers on sticky notes and stick them to the walls or desktop. It's important for the prayer requests to be visual.
- Keep a prayer journal with timelines. The prayer journal provides a history of prayer results. A prayer journal helps us see how God answered the prayers rather than going through life without noticing.
- Writing in a journal dedicates time to reflect and pushes the world aside.
- To keep focused on the prayer requests, speak out loud when praying. It helps to keep distracting thoughts out of your mind.
- As you're praying, touch or rub the sticky note or paper to raise up the person to God. It's similar to "laying hands" on the person during prayer.

The Power of prayer in the workplace — A mindset shift

Bringing prayer into my office was pivotal to my relationship with God. The top of my desk became my war room. Reading the Bible, journaling, and praying while writing sticky notes forced my mind to stay focused on God and His will for the day.

Writing the names of each company leader on sticky notes and praying over them each week helped me relax because it reinforced that God was in charge. I was His vehicle to move His kingdom forward.

The mindset shift went from the habit of praying in the car to praying as a warrior of God's army. A warrior of God's army gave perspective on difficult conversations or situations.

The importance of prayer in leadership

Starting the day in prayer starts the day on a positive note. Prayer lessens the stress that builds the closer you get to the office. Prayer keeps the focus on God's will which is the priority, over your own.

More importantly, the mindset shifts to be a warrior of God. It puts Him in control. There is a freedom in knowing that you are following His instructions. As long as the Bible is the instruction manual, prayer is constant, your mind is open to listen to His instructions, and leadership decisions and actions are easier.

Start the day in prayer

Research shows it takes an average of sixty-six days to form a habit[2]. Follow these steps for the next sixty-seven days to incorporate the habit of prayer into your day and life.

ACTIVITY: STARTING THE DAY IN PRAYER

PREPARATION

STEP 1: Reserve in your calendar 5-10 minutes at the start of the day to pray. Create a recurring meeting in your calendar and set a reminder 15 minutes prior to the appointment. Keep this appointment sacred.
STEP 2: Locate a place for prayer. Praying in your office brings God into your environment and reminds you He is with you through the day. Don't leave Jesus in the car.
STEP 3: Prepare your prayer space to avoid distractions. This includes clearing your desk of work papers, sticky notes, and anything that may distract your thoughts. Have a Bible and journal available. Use the Grace & Salt journal if you don't have another one. (www.graceandsaltbook.com/shop)
STEP 4: Set a goal. How many days per week will you pray?
STEP 5: Measurement. Track the days you pray in a spreadsheet for accountability.

Once the preparation steps are complete, go to *Prayer Steps*.

ACTIVITY: STARTING THE DAY IN PRAYER

PRAYER STEPS

STEP 1: Begin each session with prayer. It may look like this:
Dear Lord, I thank you for the opportunity to spend time in Your Word. I am Your warrior and want to do Your work. I pray for the Holy Spirit to come into my heart and mind to provide Your instructions as I read. In Jesus's name. Amen.
STEP 2: Open the Bible and start reading. Anywhere is fine. God will lead you to the message.
STEP 3: Journal throughout the session, taking notes on what speaks to you.
STEP 4: Close the session in prayer and include specific prayers for your leadership, wisdom, conversations through the day, your company, and employees.
STEP 5: Log the prayer in your measurement tracker for accountability.
Repeat steps 1-5 daily.

Lesson XII: The Power of Prayer in Leadership

"Rejoice always, pray continually, give thanks in all circumstances; for this is God's will for you in Christ Jesus." 1 Thessalonians 5:16-18[3]

SIX REASONS WHY PRAYER IS IMPORTANT TO LEADERS

1. Prayer keeps the leader focused on God and not themselves.
2. Prayer reminds the leader that God is in control.
3. Prayer provides a medium to listen to God's instructions.
4. Prayer keeps God at the top of the leader's mind.
5. Prayer keeps the leader's ego under control.
6. Prayer reinforces the leader as a warrior of God. Their purpose is to do His will. He is in control, and the leaders' role is to be His hands and feet.

SECTION II: THE LEADER: HOW TO MAINTAIN AND SURVIVE THE CHAOS SUMMARY

*C*ongratulations on investing in your self-development! It's time to celebrate!

Following is a guide to remind you of the lessons we reviewed. Feel free to print, laminate, and carry it with you.

Download it at www.graceandsaltbook.com under the resources tab.

- *VII: Temptation – Use Power for Good.*

Relationships: Keep family first. Be totally present, avoid gossip in all conversations, and forgive yourself as you forgive others. Focus your attention and power on good deeds, relationships, building trust, and spreading God's Word through your actions. Use your power for good and not evil. (Deuteronomy 6:5-9)

Focus: Don't lose focus by giving in to distractions. Pay attention to your purpose and focus on activities that move you toward your goals and purpose. When distraction arises and people lead you *from* His purpose, tell them that you are "carrying on a great project and cannot go down." (Nehemiah 6:3)

Pride: Keep pride and ego under control. Focus on servant leadership and recognize when ego leadership begins to control decisions.

- *VIII: Courage – Be Like Esther: Speak Up, Stand Up, and Step Out.* Perhaps, God brought you to this position to do His work. Be courageous. (Esther 4:13-14)
- *IX: Refresh Yourself – Have a SPA day!* To remove chaos, find a quiet place to rest your mind and body. (Mark 6:31-32)
- *X: Self-Awareness & Growth – The New You.*

The improvement plan steps are:

1. Identify which two attributes to improve
2. Identify the measurements
3. Identify current benchmarks in each attribute
4. Identify your goal (improved measurement and time frame), and
5. Tell an accountability partner. (2 Peter 1:8-11)

- *XI: Mentor – Have One, Be One.* Make disciples [of Jesus] who make disciples. Taking this one step further, mentor others as you disciple them. (Matthew 4:19-20)
- *XII: Prayer – The Power of Prayer in Leadership.* Incorporate the habit of praying into the start of your day. Bringing Jesus into the workplace is good for you and for those around you. (1 Thessalonians 5:16-18)

CLOSING THOUGHTS

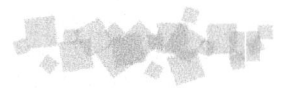

Thank you for investing in your future. My hope is for you to learn about yourself, your team, and God.

I continue to write my life story through following God's plan for me and my family. After thirty-two years in corporate America, I launched a start-up company as a career coach, professional speaker, digital online course creator, trainer, and business consultant.

I'd love to hear about your experiences and challenges. Feel free to contact me directly. My contact information is listed below.

Eventually my husband and I will retire to Wisconsin and open a tennis racquet museum. You'll need to contact me to hear about this crazy story. I think I'll always be active in helping others survive, succeed, and find joy in this world.

I look forward to hearing from you.

God bless,
Melissa

Contact Information

Melissa McCormick
e-Mail: melissa@graceandsaltbook.com
Facebook/MX3 Business Solutions
LinkedIn: www.linkedin.com/in/mccormickmelissa
Website: www.melissa-mccormick.com
Website: www.graceandsaltbook.com

MY STORY

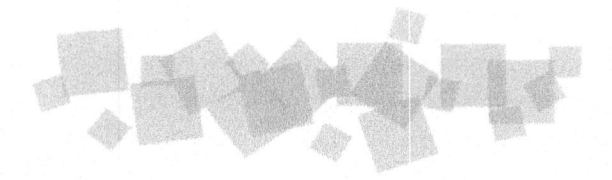

I was raised in a Christian home. Dad was a police officer, and mom worked at a bank while they raised four children. Pretty average, middle-class family in middle America. Mom took us to church on Sundays, and Dad went on holidays if he wasn't working.

Believing in Jesus wasn't an option. It was like graduating from high school. Not graduating wasn't an option. Not believing wasn't an option.

I suppose if I questioned my faith, it would have been okay. We didn't talk about faith much until my dad's heart attack.

I knew about Jesus from birth, but at twelve, I experienced Him firsthand. Dad had been sick with pneumonia. Or at least that's what the doctor thought. In reality, his heart was filling with edema, which caused a heart attack at age forty-five.

The miracle

Dad hated hospitals. He only went if someone he loved was there.

At a friend's house one night, my sister, Kathy, broke her toe. Her toe broke vertically rather than horizontally, which meant screws were surgically placed in her toe to prevent splintering.

Dad, Marvin (my oldest brother), and I went to the hospital to visit her after surgery.

Dad still wasn't feeling well but wanted to see her. Walking toward the hospital entrance, he sat down to rest. His breathing became labored.

"Marv, why don't you go ahead and find the elevator. Melissa and I will sit here for a minute," Dad said.

"Okay." And Marvin walked into the hospital lobby. *Man, this is a long line for an elevator.*

Dad got up and walked into the lobby. "Stay here," he said.

So I did. I stayed in the vestibule area of the lobby.

I watched him walk into the lobby and collapse right in front of the nurses' station. Nurses and doctors came running from everywhere.

Marvin turned around with all the commotion and found me watching the scene. He ran over to me and strategically stood in front of me to protect me from seeing what was going on. I moved slightly to the right to see exactly what was happening. I saw everything.

Dad was on a stretcher, and a doctor was literally on his chest conducting chest compressions. His hands folded in a rhythmic method counting 1 – 2 – 3, pause, 1 – 2 – 3, pause.

Doctors and nurses frantically tried to save his life while everyone stood around and watched. How incredible that the hospital hosted a doctors' conference that day! Medical assistance was available immediately.

"Doctor, do you want to call time of death?" a nurse asked.

"Wait!" Doctor Fanscali yelled. "I know him! He's my patient's father and is in his 40s. Keep going!"

1 – 2 – 3, pause, 1 – 2 – 3, pause. 20 minutes pass... 30 minutes... 35... 40 and... a heartbeat. "Finally, we have a heartbeat. Prep him and get him upstairs. Now!"

Marv and I stood there for what seemed like forever watching doctors and nurses pounding on his chest. He was dead for forty minutes with no oxygen to his brain.

Dad is reintroduced to Jesus

Dad was in intensive care for thirty days. He lost some childhood memories but lost *all* memories of church, the Bible, and of Jesus. Was this God's plan? He survived by God's hand, and God wasn't done with him yet.

Think about how crazy this story is.

- Kathy broke her toe *vertically* which caused surgery.
- Dad went to hospitals only if a family member was there.
- There are three hospitals in town. The exact hospital where my sister was recovering hosted a doctors' convention that exact day.
- The first doctor on the scene knew my dad.

None of that was a coincidence. God wasn't finished with him yet. My sister's surgeon saved Dad's life. It's unheard of to wait forty minutes to call the time of death.

When Dad recovered, he told stories that he felt peace because he knew Marlys and the kids would be okay since the life insurance was paid up.

For the next three years, Dad was home when I came home on schooldays and throughout the summer.

Once in a while, he'd ask, "Hey, Davey Gravy [that was my nickname], want to stay home from school tomorrow?"

"You bet. We can catch up on *Days of Lives!*"

His interest in Jesus heightened, and he started studying the Bible. God's timing was perfect. Both Dad and I studied the Bible together. He had a new interest, and I was attending confirmation classes. Studying together was pretty awesome.

Dad passed away on August 6, 1981. Although I was sixteen when he died, I'm forever grateful to God for giving me three more years with him.

College and church

The bitter cold wind whips through my hair while my girlfriends and I walk downtown in this small Iowa town. So much snow. Main Street is lined with shops, bars, and the Decorah State Bank.

"Hey, let's go in here. They have nice clothes, and we can warm up."

As I reach for the door handle, a man swoops in and opens it for me. Startled, I jump back. "Let me get that for you," he said. "Oh! Okay. How nice!" He wasn't even going into the store. *This is the school for me! I love this town!*

I chose Luther College in Decorah, IA because a man opened the door for me unexpectedly. And...it has a high scholastic reputation and ranking.

My faith wasn't a priority in college. I believed in Jesus but that was it. I figured that one day I'd go back to church and to the foundation Mom and Dad instilled. At that time, being a Christian was going to church on Sundays.

Marriage and church

"Melissa and Terry called. They want us to come over to watch the Bears-Packers game today," I told Mike, my boyfriend.

"Okay. Sounds good. Tell them we'll be there," Mike said.

"Great. I'll take the garbage out and be right back."

I'm glad he has a ground-level apartment. So much easier using the sliding patio doors than walking up and down the stairs with garbage bags.

I toss the garbage bags in the dumpster and head back in. The apartment is small, and the living room barely has enough room for two people to pass.

Mike pulls me on his lap. "Hey, what are you doing?" I ask.

Holding a ring box, he hesitates before he says, "Will you marry me?"

Oh my. This is it. It's happening.

We've been dating for almost four years, and I've been sending subtle or not-so-subtle hints for months. We'd gone ring shopping, but I didn't know if he was seriously going to ask me.

"YES! Of course!"

It was the best Bears-Packers game ever. I don't even remember who won!

Planning for the wedding was fantastic. I wasn't too particular on the details except for one. I wanted to be married at my childhood church by my childhood pastor.

Wedding day

Waking up early on a warm November day, I quickly get dressed and drive to Diane's to style my hair and veil. The cemetery is forty minutes from Diane's so I better get moving to make sure I get to the church on time.

I pull into the cemetery and find the family plots under the big oak tree at the top of the hill. Mom bought a nice granite bench after Dad died so we could sit and talk to him when visiting. This morning I was in a hurry but needed to stop by for a few words of wisdom.

It was so beautiful, standing there, thinking about Dad and wishing he were here as the wind whipped my veil around. I slowly walk back to the car and see another car drive through the cemetery.

They probably think my fiancé was killed and I haven't recovered.

I laugh and say, "Gotta go, Dad. Love you."

The church is filled with friends and family. The anticipation and excitement fill the room. Mike and I stand at the altar holding hands.

Ouch! That hurts! He's crushing my hand. Why is the pastor telling this story? That's odd and isn't appropriate for our wedding day. Where did this come from? No wonder Mike's squeezing my hand. Okay, let's get through this and off to the reception.

Our wedding day experience prolonged my hiatus from church until the birth of our daughter four years later.

Children and church

Raising our children in a church was non-negotiable. So I forgave the pastor and regularly attended my childhood church for the next twenty years.

Pastors came and went. And my faith grew stronger and stronger through my leadership roles in the youth group, puppet ministry, and the annual mission trips. We raised Amanda and Nick to love Jesus and follow His lessons.

In 2015, the pull to do something more became very strong. Up to that point, Mike's involvement was supporting us behind the scenes. He didn't actively participate in church.

"I think it's time that I get more involved in church," he said, out of the blue.

"What? Are you serious?" *I've waited twenty years to hear him say those words.*

"Yes, I'm serious. But I want to find a new church."

"Okay. Absolutely."

Was God pulling me to another church or to something new? Did He want me out of my comfort zone to disciple others? Perhaps He was using Mike to get my attention.

An exit strategy was established and implemented. After my final duty was complete, we started looking for a church.

"Don't forget Thursday night is Nick's baccalaureate service," I said.

The auditorium is quiet and filled with anticipation while parents and graduates listen to the message. Pastor Wayne Hume was the keynote speaker.

"Hey, Mom, that's Grant's dad," Nick whispers. I smile and nod.

Driving home from the service, we were quiet in thought.

Suddenly, Mike says, "How about Pastor Hume's church? We could go on Sunday to check it out. I liked his message a lot."

And the rest is history. It was the only church we visited. We were home.

Relationships and church

Untangling myself from my responsibilities and connections at my childhood church would be tricky but no different than strategically executing a succession plan in a business. The goal was to minimize the gaps. It was important to not burn any bridges. After all, we weren't getting a divorce.

God and church

Prior to leaving my childhood church, church had become an institution to me. It became a corporation filled with rules and politics, and that was not what God intended. Toward the end, my role was filled with stress, and I knew it was time for me to leave.

God used people around me to get my attention. Leaving my childhood church was difficult for me, my family, and friends. But Northeast's [our new church] mission aligned with my new goals and was an organization trying to remove the institution-type bureaucratic atmosphere from God and Jesus.

From the depth of my soul, I know God grafted me from my childhood church to Northeast. I am to take the experience and knowledge I gained at my childhood church and utilize those skills at Northeast.

I thank everyone throughout my life who gave me opportunities to grow in my faith and gave me freedom to create a strong youth group while trying new things without the fear of failure.

God's grafting exercise wasn't finished. I continued to pray at work daily for my company, Taylor, and its leadership. I decided to pursue a Master of Science degree in organizational leadership from Southern New Hampshire University in late 2017. Through my studies, I became interested in leadership development. Through the master's program's courses, God grafted me again from Taylor to my next calling. Finish my book, share my story, and pay forward what I learned through Taylor, my mentors, my childhood church, and my wonderful husband and children.

I left Taylor Company on April 26, 2019, after thirty-two years of service. It wouldn't have been possible without the never-ending support of my husband and family.

I know what I am supposed to do, but I don't know where it will lead me.

Isaiah 6:8 says, "Then I heard the voice of the Lord saying, 'Whom shall I send? And who will go for us?' And I said, 'Here I am. Send me!'"

Here I am—trusting that God continues to reveal His plan to me.

Trust in God.

Listen to His voice.

Follow and believe.

ENDNOTES

Lesson I: Grace & Salt

1. The NIV Study Bible. (1995) 10th anniversary edition. Grand Rapids, MI Zondervan p. 1819.
2. "History of salt." (n.d.). Retrieved from https://www.seasalt.com/history-of-salt
3. Anushka, F. (2018, Oct 3). 55 Surprisingly SMART uses for salt. Retrieved from https://experthometips.com/smart-uses-for-salt
4. "History of salt". (n.d.). Retrieved from https://www.seasalt.com/history-of-salt

Lesson II: Connections & Sense of Belonging

1. Allen K., and Kern, P. (June 2019). The Importance of Belonging Across Life. Psychology Today. (para 1) Retrieved from https://www.psychologytoday.com/us/blog/sense-belonging/201906/the-importance-belonging-across-life
2. Osborne, S., Hammond, M., (2017). Effective Employee Engagement in the Workplace. International Journal of Applied Management and Technology. Vol 16, Issue 1, Pages 50-67.
3. Newstrom, J. (2015). *Organizational Behavior: Human Behavior at Work*, 14th Edition, New York, NY: McGraw Hill.
4. "Job Training & Career Counseling Industry in the US – Market Research Report". (May 24, 2021) Retrieved from https://www.ibisworld.com/united-states/market-research-reports/job-training-career-counseling-industry/
5. U.S. Bureau of Labor Statistics. (n.d.) Retrieved from https://www.bls.gov/ooh/Community-and-Social-Service/School-and-career-counselors.htm
6. Newstrom, J. (2015). *Organizational Behavior: Human Behavior at Work*, 14th Edition, New York, NY: McGraw Hill.

Lesson III: Serving & Giving

1. Center for Servant Leadership. (n.d.) The servant as leader. Retrieved from https://www.greenleaf.org/what-is-servant-leadership/
2. Dean, Jeremy. (2009). "How Long to Form a Habit?" Retrieved from https://www.spring.org.uk/2009/09/how-long-to-form-a-habit.php
3. "The History of Teflon, Fluoropolymers. An Accidental Discovery". (n.d.) Retrieved from https://www.teflon.com/en/news-events/history

Lesson IV: Remove Inactive Yeast Swiftly

1. "How long does yeast last?" (n.d.). Retrieved from: https://www.eatbydate.com/other/baking/yeast/

Lesson V: Planting Seeds & Fishing

1. The Serenity Prayer by Reinhold Niebuhr. (December 1, 2019). Retrieved from https://www.commonprayers.org/the-serenity-prayer/
2. Center for Servant Leadership. (n.d.) The servant as leader. Retrieved from https://www.greenleaf.org/what-is-servant-leadership/
3. "Our History". (n.d.). The Colgate Company. Retrieved from https://www.colgatepalmolive.com/en-us/who-we-are/history
4. Colgate Annual Report 2020 (n.d.) Retrieved from https://investor.colgatepalmolive.com/static-files/1d8483af-a8b5-485f-9cff-992592a92b3b
5. Covey, S. (2006). *The Speed of Trust*. Free Press. New York, NY.
6. Covey, S. (2006). *The Speed of Trust*. Free Press. New York, NY.

Lesson VI: Pray Until Something Happens (PUSH)

1. The NIV Study Bible. (1995) 10th anniversary edition. Grand Rapids, MI Zondervan p. 1821.
2. Gieschen, C. A. (2008). Christian Identity in Pagan Thessalonica: The Imitation of Paul's cruciform life. Concordia Theological Quarterly 72, 3-18.
3. Holy Bible. NIV. (2011). Retrieved from https://www.biblegateway.com

Lesson VII: Temptation — Use Your Power for Good

1. "balance". 2020. Merriam-Webster.com. Retrieved from https://www.merriam-webster.com/dictionary/balance
2. What is forgiveness? (n.d.). Psychology Today. Retrieved from https://www.psychologytoday.com/us/basics/forgiveness
3. What is forgiveness? (n.d.). Psychology Today. Retrieved from https://www.psychologytoday.com/us/basics/forgiveness
4. All About God. (n.d.). Forgiving yourself. Retrieved from www.allaboutgod.com/forgiving-yourself.htm
5. Orr, James, M.A., D.D. General Editor. "Entry for 'CUPBEARER.'" "International Standard Bible Encyclopedia," 1915.
6. "Nehemiah" (n.d.). Retrieved from https://en.wikipedia.org/wiki/Nehemiah
7. 10 facts about the Colosseum. National Geographic Kids. (n.d.). Retrieved from https://www.natgeokids.com/uk/discover/history/romans/colosseum/
8. How many people did it take to build the Roman colosseum? Retrieved from https://www.quora.com/How-many-people-did-it-take-to-build-the-Roman-Colosseum

9. Hadrian's Wall. History Channel. (2018, Jan). Retrieved from https://www.history.com/topics/ancient-rome/hadrians-wall
10. Ephron, N. (director) & Ephron, D. (producer). (1998). You've Got Mail [Motion picture]. United States: Warner Brothers.

Lesson VIII: Courage — Be Like Esther: Stand Up, Speak Up, and Step Out

1. Encyclopedia.com. (n.d.). Esther. Retrieved from https://www.encyclopedia.com/philosophy-and-religion/bible/old-testament/esther

Lesson IX: Refresh Yourself — Have a SPA (Spiritual Personal Activity) Day!

1. 10 Quotes from Billy Graham on Rest. (November 8, 2019). Retrieved from: https://billygrahamlibrary.org/blog-10-quotes-from-billy-graham-on-rest/

Lesson X: Self-Awareness & Growth — The New You

1. Holy Bible. NIV. (2011). Retrieved from https://www.biblegateway.com
2. Holy Bible. NIV. (2011). Retrieved from https://www.biblegateway.com

Lesson XI: Mentor - Have One, Be One

1. Holy Bible. NIV. (2011). Retrieved from https://www.biblegateway.com
2. Zhang, H., Isaac, A., Wright, E., Alrajhi, Y., & Seikaly, H. (2017). Formal mentorship in a surgical residency training program: a prospective interventional study. *Journal of Otolaryngology – Head of Neck Surgery*. DOI 10.1186/s40463-017-0186-2
3. Dictionary.com. (n.d.) Retrieved from https://www.dictionary.com/browse/mentor
4. Runyan, C., Austen, J. & Gildenblatt, L. (2017). Mentorship During Transitions. American Psychological Association. Vol. 35, No. 4, 508-510. Retrieved from http://dx.doi.org/10.1037/fsh0000284
5. Runyan, C., Austen, J. & Gildenblatt, L. (2017). Mentorship During Transitions. American Psychological Association. Vol. 35, No. 4, 508-510. Retrieved from http://dx.doi.org/10.1037/fsh0000284
6. Covey, S. (2006). *The Speed of Trust*. Free Press. New York, NY.
7. Covey, S. (2006). *The Speed of Trust*. Free Press. New York, NY.
8. Inzer, L.D and Crawford, C.B. (2005). A Review of Formal and Informal Mentoring: Processes, Problems, and Design. Journal of Leadership Education, vol. 4, (1).
9. Inzer, L.D and Crawford, C.B. (2005). A Review of Formal and Informal Mentoring: Processes, Problems, and Design. Journal of Leadership Education, vol. 4, (1).
10. Holy Bible. NIV. (2011). Retrieved from https://www.biblegateway.com
11. Holy Bible. NIV. (2011). Retrieved from https://www.biblegateway.com

12. Holy Bible. NIV. (2011). Retrieved from https://www.biblegateway.com

Lesson XII: The Power of Prayer in Leadership

1. Holy Bible. NIV. (2011). Retrieved from https://www.biblegateway.com
2. Rubin, G. (Oct 2009). How long to form a habit? Psychology Today. Retrieved from https://www.psychologytoday.com/us/blog/the-happiness-project/200910/stop-expecting-change-your-habit-in-21-days
3. Holy Bible. NIV. (2011). Retrieved from https://www.biblegateway.com

ACKNOWLEDGMENTS

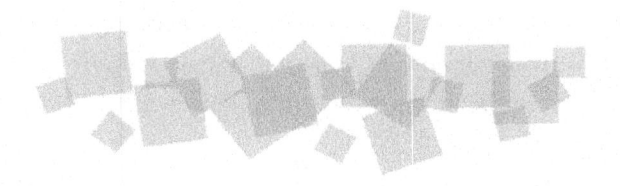

Having a cheering section on the sidelines is what powers great athletes to perform against all odds. My cheering section has been cheering loudly and proudly every step of the way.

Thank you for believing in me—Mike McCormick (the best husband in the world), Amanda (McCormick) Lantz (daughter), Shawn Lantz (son-in-law), Nick McCormick (son), Caitlyn Schneeman (future daughter-in-law), Marlys Mackey Marsh (mom), Kathy Panozzo, Karen Mackey, Carla Mackey (sisters), and Marv Mackey and Jeff Mackey (brothers). And Dad, thank you for guiding me from Heaven. I love you.

Tricia Bennett, what a blessing you have been in my life! Your never-ending encouragement, support, laughter, and tears are what's kept me pushing forward all of these years. Thank you for always being there through the ups and downs. I love you.

Melissa (Missy) Wolfe. How can I put into words what your support and friendship has meant to me? Your insight, advice, faith, and unconditional love are a few ways you've impacted my life and direction. Starting and growing our businesses together has been so much fun. I can't wait to see what's next for us. Team Melissa rules!

God introduced me to Joan Drop on a mission trip to the Dominican Republic. I thank Him for our friendship every day. Joan, thank you for being there for me no matter what. For believing in me. For betting on me. For pushing me to finish this book.

Nisha Gupta, my dear friend, coach, and business collaborator. Thank you for helping me realize my goals. Finishing this book and starting a business were scary but with you by my side, it's been fun and rewarding. Thank you for challenging me every step of the way. From an iD to a D, you have a special place in my heart and life.

Thank you, Pamela Jean, Dee Hudson, and Nicole Lupushansky, my Accountability Pod ladies, for walking this journey with me. Or running in our cases. Your unending, unconditional support personally and professionally have been overwhelming. I love our Power Hours. Let's keep spreading His joy and Word.

Thank you to the Grace & Salt First Readers club; Joe Barrett, Tricia Bennett, Dave Boden, Barb Clausen, Joan Drop, Matt Guevara, Nisha Gupta, Wayne Hume, Emily Krantz, Amanda Lantz, Shawn Lantz, Mike McCormick, Nick McCormick, Kathy Panozzo, Stephanie Panozzo, Caitlyn Schneeman, and Melissa (Missy) Wolfe. Finding time to read Grace & Salt and provide valuable input and insight was appreciated beyond words. I hope the final product meets your expectations. We've come a long way from that first draft in 2019.

My first mentor and friend, Clark Wangaard, shaped me in so many ways. Clark, thank you for being the best mentor and boss a gal could ever ask for. I'm forever indebted to you for reminding me to keep business personal and thank you for all you've done for me and my family.

Courage, wisdom, and heart make a great boss and leader! And that's my dear friend, Jeremy Dobrowolski. I couldn't have done any of it without you, your support, encouragement, and heart. Thank you.

Joe Barrett. Thank you for your friendship, guidance, and support over the past twenty years and especially for this book. God put us together and it's been amazing from the first telephone call to birthday dinners, and special lunches. What an amazing ride! I'm looking forward to many more years of challenging discussions and celebrating our successes.

To my friends at Taylor, the distributors, and customers. You all have a special place in my heart. Thank you for supported me through this journey. Enjoy Hotel California!

Thank you to the countless friends who have supported me. Gave me encouragement when I was ready to shred everything and cheered me on when I held my breath. Amazing and overwhelming!

Having a pastor who becomes a friend and advisor is special. Thank you, Wayne Hume, for encouraging me to seek a relationship with Jesus through this book and for your dedication and passion to spread God's messages through relationships and community.

To Mary Kay Morrison, author of *Legacy of Laughter*. Thank you for your advice and unconditionally welcoming me into your life. You are amazing!

Jesus put the right people in my path at the right time. Thank you, Dan Domberg, Megan Ryan, Wayne Hume, Matt Guevara, Emily Krantz, She Speaks Conference, Ginny Yttrup, Amanda Luedeke, Jenneth Dyck, Leslie McKee, Ben Wolf, Mary Kay Morrison and Carson Cuevas.

Who will He bring next? 2 Corinthians 9:8 (NIV)

ABOUT THE AUTHOR

Entry-level to executive describes Melissa's journey in corporate America. Through her thirty plus years she learned how to navigate up and through the organization from early days shipping equipment overseas to the senior vice president of global sales, service, and marketing. Today, Melissa is a career coach, speaker, writer, and trainer helping women reach their full potential through enhancing communication, negotiation, and leadership skills. She credits her success to Jesus and family who have been with her every step of this journey.

Melissa continues to serve on the mission committee at Northeast Christian Church. Leading, serving and supporting partnerships in the Dominican Republic and around the world are what drives and motivates her. She holds leadership roles in Rotary International District 6420, and is an active member of the Rockford Chamber of Commerce.

Be sure to check out her digital course, *Break Free from the Career Comfort Zone* that guides women to their "happy place" where passions and skills intersect. Interested? If so, this self-guided course helps to identify and validate your purpose, align it with your career, and provide direction for what's next as well as teach communication skills to speak up and step out. Learn more at www.melissa-mccormick.com.

Melissa has been recognized as a 2020 Stateline Women in Business honoree and received the 2021 Better Business Bureau Torch Award for marketplace ethics in the women-owned business category.

Her first priority continues to be her family and spreading the joy of Jesus.